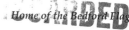

THE UNION
DIVIDED

Mark E. Neely, Jr.

THE UNION DIVIDED

PARTY CONFLICT

IN THE

CIVIL WAR

NORTH

HARVARD UNIVERSITY PRESS

Cambridge, Massachusetts and London, England 2002

Library of Congress Cataloging-in-Publication Data

Neely, Mark E.
The union divided : party conflict in the Civil War North/Mark E. Neely, Jr.
p. cm.
Includes bibliographical references and index.
ISBN 0-674-00742-5 (alk. paper)
1. Political parties—United States—History—19th century.
2. United States—Politics and government—1861–1865.   I. Title.

JK2260 .N445 2002
320.973′09′034—dc21
2001039873

CONTENTS

PREFACE

I FIRST GREW CURIOUS about the Civil War and the two-party system in the 1980s while I was investigating the military arrests of civilians in the North during the Civil War. It took me years to complete the research and writing for what became *The Fate of Liberty: Abraham Lincoln and Civil Liberties,* and along the way I gave various papers across the country on the subject, based on my preliminary findings. When I finished a presentation, often someone in the audience would ask a leading question: Didn't I think that the existence of a two-party system in the North helped make President Lincoln's tough policies on civil liberties more acceptable to the American people?

I knew they were expecting a "yes" answer, but I always had trouble giving it. Their expectations stemmed from the exalted reputation of the two-party system among historians and political scientists who took it as an article of faith that the continued competition of parties in the North during the Civil War proved advantageous—even crucial—to the success of the Union war effort. I would hem and haw and ramble, reluctant to look unread in the recent literature on political history but never really understanding in my own mind how party competition *helped*. I am literal-minded, and to me the Republicans defended the commander-in-chief and the Democrats criticized him, and it was a zero-sum game.

I was dissatisfied with my responses and with the answer expected of me, but I could not stop to work on the problem directly. I returned to the subject of political parties in the war fortuitously. Not long after I finished *The Fate of Liberty,* Gabor S. Boritt asked me to prepare a paper on the Battle of Chancellorsville for the Civil War Institute at Gettysburg College. By way of preparation, I decided to read all the letters written to Abraham Lincoln for the period from General Joseph Hooker's appointment as commander of the Army of the Potomac through the time of the battle itself, roughly the first five months of 1863. In the course of that research I happened upon a couple of sets of resolutions sent from Illinois regiments to President Lincoln denouncing party strife and vowing to return home to disperse the legislature at Springfield if ordered. I was staggered by the discovery, never having seen the like in some twenty years of reading and writing about the political and constitutional history of the United States in the nineteenth century.

The resolutions, since they came from military units, seemed to me a palpable threat and offered evidence that party competition was not only unhelpful but at times downright threatening to the republic. My initial dissatisfaction with the reigning theory of party conflict now led to research directly on the subject, and on October 16, 1993, I presented a paper on "The Civil War and the Two-Party System" at a Huntington Library symposium for the opening of its exhibit called "The Last Best Hope of Earth: Abraham Lincoln and the Promise of America." The essay subsequently appeared in a book assembling the conference papers called *"We Cannot Escape History": Lincoln and the Last Best Hope of Earth,* edited by James M. McPherson and published by the University of Illinois Press. But I wasn't through with the subject.

I spent the year 1997–1998 at the Huntington Library in San Marino, California, working on the problem, reading manuscripts and newspapers. But when I came to Penn State afterward I still lacked a key ingredient: I was convinced that the two-party system was not a decisive advantage to the northern cause in the Civil War, but I had no *positive* explanation for what happened in northern politics during the war.

Then, in the spring term of 2000 the history department gave me my first opportunity to teach American constitutional history. That caused me to think long and hard about the Constitution again. It also caused me to think in more positive ways about the Constitution than the subject of military arrests of civilians had done back in the 1980s. Increasingly, I followed the advice of the constitutional historian Harold M. Hyman, in *A More Perfect Union: The Impact of the Civil War and Reconstruction on the Constitution,* to consider the way the Constitution shaped the war, rather than the other way around. And it dawned on me what a possible solution to the problem was. This book is the result.

IN PREVIOUS BOOKS, such as *The Fate of Liberty,* I built the text on neglected archival sources, aiming at exhaustive research in those sources and at definitive conclusions based upon them. The method in this book is necessarily entirely different. There is no exhausting the sources on northern politics in the Civil War. Moreover, many of the crucial sources are familiar to other historians—the letters written to Abraham Lincoln, for example, or editorials in the New York *Tribune*. I could not entertain hope of reaching definitive conclusions on such a subject. This book is meant to be more tentative and suggestive. It is meant to open the subject, not to be the final word on it.

In the past, I have slighted research in newspapers. I now recollect my graduate training in history in the 1960s as in part an exercise in demonstrating the limitations of newspapers as sources of nineteenth-century public opinion. Such use was gradually abandoned when historians recognized the determined partisanship and rigid partiality of the period's press.

But what makes newspapers useless as barometers of public opinion—their blind partisanship—makes them essential to research in political history. Indeed, they were political history and little else. For me, they have made the political events of the Civil War era come alive once again. They restore an exciting sense of contingency, remind us of forgotten episodes, and help us to return to the mindset of the era.

So, of course, does the manuscript correspondence of the politicians consulted for this book. Because there were no telephones, nineteenth-century politicians had to write letters about nearly every problem they faced—no matter how delicate. The resulting letters are striking for their candor, therefore, and also help to restore a proper sense of the stakes for which they played. The excellent rag-paper on which they wrote has survived nicely to our own day, and the brutal standards of unregulated political competition in the era created a political culture in which retaining such letters and risking their perusal by posterity did not bother the politicians as much as it might today. Nothing so much enlivens a day in the archives as encountering a letter with the words "burn this" written at the top.

MUCH OF THE RESEARCH for this book I completed as the R. Stanton Avery Fellow at the Huntington Library in San Marino, California, in 1997–1998. I am indebted to Robert Ritchie, Director of Research at the Huntington, and to the rest of the library's staff for indispensable help in developing this book.

In October 2000 I presented part of the manuscript of the book at the Civil War Era workshop at Penn State, and I benefited from comments by the director of the Civil War Era Center William Blair and Robert Sandow, who is writing about resistance to the war in Pennsylvania. Valuable suggestions and challenges also came from the other participants in the seminar.

In the late spring of 2001 Daniel W. Crofts of the College of New Jersey read the whole manuscript and sent me pages of constructive criticism, to which I have attempted to do justice. I owe him a big debt for the help. I have received useful criticism and advice as well from Jean Baker, Gordon Wood, William Gienapp, and Alice Fahs. Sylvia Neely criticized, encouraged, and formatted when I most needed each.
September 2001

THE UNION
DIVIDED

INTRODUCTION

"If the loyal people, *united*, were put to the utmost of their strength by the rebellion, must they not fail when *divided*, and partially paralized, by a political war among themselves?"

ABRAHAM LINCOLN, *November 10, 1864*

AFTER HIS SUCCESSFUL REELECTION in 1864, President Lincoln could not help reflecting momentarily on the fearful uncertainties of two-party competition in the midst of rebellion. He acknowledged the anxiety, commonly felt in the previous months, that a presidential election might divide the political house in the North and paralyze the Union war effort. But he quickly moved on to affirm that "the election was a necessity." After all, he was addressing from a window of the White House a group of well-wishers celebrating his victory at the polls, and the statement was one in a long line made by presidents-elect to heal divisions created by political campaigns. Free government was not possible without elections, Lincoln pointed out, and the "strife of the election" he could now dismiss philosophically as "but human-nature practically applied to the facts of the case."[1]

To focus on these conciliatory remarks about the opposition party is misleading because they were spoken after the election was decided. The tone of the electoral campaign had been different. Lincoln, though the presidential candidate, had not taken an active public role in the canvass. Campaigning was thought to be beneath the dignity of presidential candidates, especially incumbents, and public appearances and speaking were left to others in the party. The keynote speech for Lincoln's reelection campaign was given by Secretary of State William H. Seward, and it struck a different note.

Though often called the "Auburn Speech" because Seward gave it in his home town, Auburn, New York, the actual title of the address was "The Allies of Treason." Seward spoke on September 3, 1864, shortly after news arrived that the Democrats had nominated George B. McClellan for president at Chicago and that Atlanta had fallen to General William T. Sherman. The military victory made it an "auspicious . . . occasion," but, Seward said, the event had "nevertheless failed to bring out some whom we might have expected here." What kept them away from the rally was "party spirit."[2]

Seward considered "the recommendations of the Convention at Chicago as tending to subvert the Republic." "It will seem a hard thing," he admitted, "when I imply that a party, like the democratic party, can either meditate or inconsiderately adopt measures to overthrow the Republic. All experience, however, shows that it is by the malice or the madness of great parties that free states have been brought down to destruction."[3] Citing documents printed in the London

Times as proof, the secretary of state declared that the opposition's "nomination and . . . platform . . . were made by treaty formally contracted between the democratic traitors at Richmond, and the democratic opposition at Chicago, signed, sealed, attested, and delivered."[4]

Thus, the Republicans appear to have been a good deal more unnerved by party opposition before the election turned out favorably than afterward. And even after, Lincoln offered only words of philosophic resignation. He did not give a resounding affirmation of the benefits of two-party competition to the country. The president's measured and heartfelt statement, let alone Seward's forthright expression of alarm, seems a long way from the confidence exuded by modern historians that, as one of them has put it, "the North had a decisive advantage over the South because it continued to have a two-party rivalry during the war while the Confederacy did not."[5] Another modern historian has gone so far as to say that political "turmoil" in the North during the Civil War actually "strengthened the government."[6] The Civil War president, on the other hand, had his doubts about the contribution of party strife to the war effort. Lincoln avowed—and he was in a position to know— that "a presidential election occurring in regular course during the rebellion added not a little to the strain" on the republic's strength.[7] And Seward had more than implied that the opposition was allied to treason.

Certainly Americans today are grateful that the two-party system survived the war, but we should not allow that somewhat self-congratulatory point to lead us uncritically to the very different conclusion that the party system was an unalloyed advantage the North enjoyed over the South, even "a *decisive* advantage," as Michael F. Holt, the dean of American political historians, believes. Yet over the last generation of writing on the American Civil War, historians of northern politics have found surprising unanimity in their belief that the two-party system operated entirely to the North's advantage.[8]

This enthusiastic agreement on the utility of two-party politics in the war has offered a pat answer to a difficult question, stilling rather than stimulating the writing of Civil War political history. It would be difficult today to find a practicing historian of northern politics who does not believe in the two-party-system theory, as it might be called, but it would be equally difficult to find one contented with the recent output of scholarship on the political history of the war. It has been sadly neglected. As Holt has put it in a recent assessment of the field, "Since the mid-1960s"—the very era in which the two-party-system theory emerged—"the only general overview has been James A. Rawley's valuable, but brief and unannotated, *The Politics of Union,* published in 1974."[9] Curiosity was obviously stifled.

Taking my cue from Lincoln rather than the historians, I have written this book to liberate the study of Civil War politics in the North from the deadening cliché of overconfidence in the two-party system in nineteenth-century America. I want to restore a sense of wonder at the astonishing political conflicts that emerged within the North during the war. We need to explain, I think, the sense of alarm expressed by Seward as the very keynote of the 1864 campaign, and recall to mind the high risks politicians were willing to take with the future of the republic in order to ensure their own fortunes.

To assess for the first time the alleged decisive advantage held by the North over the South in the Civil War because of its "continued . . . two-party rivalry during the war" will constitute the central and major preoccupation of this book. It is not yet possible to provide a comparative analysis of northern and southern politics during the war. Like the "elusive synthesis" of northern politics Holt cries out for, such a comparison is well beyond the reach of scholarship on the period now. In fact, such a comparison is impossible for the very reason that there is no modern synthesis and widely accepted "general overview" of northern politics during the war.

The work that is emerging on politics and nation-building in the Confederacy is suggestive, however. George C. Rable, in his book *The Confederate Republic: A Revolution against Politics,* has expressed skepticism about the purported advantages of a two-party system in the Civil War. He is convinced that southerners, under the dire circumstances imposed by the war, were dead-set against creating a new party system and likely faced insuperable obstacles to forming parties anyhow. He is not at all sure that the consequent absence of parties in the Confederacy posed a formidable handicap to their war effort, and in speculative asides he expresses his doubts about the parties' usefulness to the North.[10] Richard Bensel is likewise skeptical of the application of the theory to the Confederacy, as he sees the emergence of a surprisingly strong central state there and finds it logically improbable that the opposition to the Confederate government was somehow more powerful for want of organization. As for the northern war effort, Bensel suggests that reliance on party kept the administration from forming a bureaucratic administrative apparatus and left it reliant on private industry for economic mobilization.[11]

These are powerfully suggestive critiques, but their approach is oblique, and general belief in the idea that the two-party system aided the North to victory has survived their works. The acid test must come in looking directly at the politics of the North, where parties did persist to shape and debate the war effort. And the two-party-system theory (its origins, history, and logic) must be directly addressed as well—which will be done in the last chapter of this book. Though an altogether satisfactory political history of the North in the Civil War may not yet be available, we must take first steps first, however tentative. And indeed this book is meant to be tentative and suggestive. I mean mostly to re-place pat answers with questions and to stimulate debate. I have few pat answers of my own.

1

"No party now but all for our country"

POLITICAL PARTIES AND THE PUBLIC SAFETY

WHEN THE CIVIL WAR BEGAN, a two-party
system had not functioned in the United States for seven
years. The 1856 presidential election saw a three-way contest,
with Democrat James Buchanan emerging as victor. Four
years later Republican Abraham Lincoln won the presidency
with but 40 percent of the popular vote in a four-way contest. The old Democratic party split into southern and
northern branches with separate presidential tickets and
platforms in 1860; and one of the parties formed for the election of 1856, the American or Know Nothing party, disappeared and was replaced by the Constitutional Union party.
At the state level, new parties with new names had come and
gone or remained in trace form here and there. Thus, American voters had little reason to think of the United States the
way we tend to now, as a country distinguished by a two-
party political system, featuring stable contests between
well-run national organizations with long traditions at their
backs.

Whether most Americans in the middle of the nineteenth
century thought two-party competition in times of peace

was normal, let alone beneficial, is not clear.[1] Conclusive evidence is lacking: in that innocent time before the dawning of social science, not many people were prompted to say anything either way. Universities did not employ political analysts to study the problem in the abstract; newspaper editorial writers were fiercely partisan and sought to help one party and hurt the opposition, not to analyze or even celebrate the "system"; and ordinary people tended to accept the presence of political parties on the scene without much thought. Casual shifting in assumptions about the nature of party competition was common even in the ardently partisan press. Thus, when the Chicago *Tribune,* just after the fall of Fort Sumter, called for an end to partisanship for the duration of the war, the editor wrote, "We no longer ask—Is he a Republican? Is he a Democrat?" Those questions had their roots in an assumption that the two parties were normal fixtures in peace. But only a day later, the same newspaper, cautioning Republicans against partisanship, assumed the presence of many parties: "We are not, henceforth, Republicans, Democrats, Americans, Old Line Whigs, Conservatives or Abolitionists." The *Tribune* thus contradicted itself in a way, but probably convictions on the matter did not run very deep on either day.[2]

How many parties seemed normal to Americans after the bewildering experience of the tumultuous 1850s is not clear, but one thing is certain: most Americans expected parties to cease operation if the country were invaded or faced a major rebellion—the emergencies contemplated in Article I, section 9 of the United States Constitution (providing in such crises for suspending the writ of habeas corpus). The assumption that political parties had no role in times of invasion or rebellion was a legacy from the founders of the country. Number 50 of the famous *Federalist* papers, for example, stated that "an extinction of parties necessarily implies either a universal alarm for the public safety, or an absolute extinction of liberty."[3] The founders' disapproval of political parties in general may have substantially lost its influence among politically active Americans by the middle of the nineteenth century, but the idea that parties had no proper role in times of national emergency persisted.

Even the era's major intellectual champion of political parties as institutions essential to republics changed his mind dramatically when the country faced rebellion. Francis Lieber, a professor at Columbia College in New York City by the time of the Civil War, had given rare systematic analysis to the question. As early as 1839, in a pioneering work called *Manual of Political Ethics* Lieber had concluded that history offered "no instance of a free state without parties," and it was not "desirable that no parties should exist." "Without parties," he contended, "there could be no loyal, steady, lasting and effective opposition, one of the surest safeguards of public peace . . . Without parties many of the wisest measures could never be carried, and many of the best intended measures would remain harsh, unmodified, absolute."[4]

But Lieber had always had reservations about the role of political parties in war. In the *Manual of Political Ethics* he had qualified his position on the "great question how far an opposition ought not only to yield, after war has once been declared, but, to aid patriotically in carrying it to a glorious end."

> If your *nation* engages in the war, and not simply a preposterous *administration,* against your opinion, you may act as private citizen as you like,

provided always you do in no sort or manner aid
directly or indirectly the enemy . . . but if you are
a representative or officer, you are bound first of
all to bring the war to a happy and glorious end,
and not to cripple the administration. The latter
could be treasonable. Remember that it is your
state, your nation, that declares and fights out
the war, not this or that minister; remember that
the honor and history of your country are en-
gaged; that however conscientious you may be in
your opposition you may err after all; that you
cannot oppose the administration without
strengthening the enemy, who has unsheathed
his sword against your kindred, and that whatever your opinion was as to the beginning of the
war, all considerations absolutely cease, when the
enemy approaches your own country . . . If an opposition feels really and conscientiously convinced that the war is inexpedient, let them follow the old Roman rule: treat after victory, but
fight until then.[5]

Lieber was an old soldier himself, and faced with the outbreak of the rebellion in 1861, he altered his earlier pro-party
positions and by 1863 wrote a pamphlet entitled *No Party
Now but All for Our Country*. In it he insisted:

Parties are unavoidable in free countries, and may
be useful if they acknowledge the country far
above themselves, and remain within the sanctity
of the fundamental law . . . But Party has no
meaning in far the greater number of the highest

and the common relations of human life. When
we are ailing, we do not take medicine by party
prescription. We do not pursue truth, or cultivate
science, by party dogmas; and we do not, we must
not, love and defend our country and our liberty
. . . according to party rules.[6]

Lieber never spoke well of parties again.[7]

Abraham Lincoln was a party politician all his adult life.
He openly acknowledged that, in ordinary times, a "man
who is of neither party, is not—cannot be, of any consequence." Nevertheless, Lincoln knew when to draw the line.
In his eulogy on Henry Clay in 1852, Lincoln said, "A free people, in times of peace and quiet—when pressed by no common danger—naturally divide into parties."[8] He never said
exactly what would obtain when a free people *were* pressed
by common danger, but the implication of his belief seems
obvious—that parties would be unnatural in time of rebellion or invasion.

The actual political history of the country somewhat
defied that assumption, as it had some other assumptions
behind the mechanisms established by the Constitution, but
the collapse of the Federalist party as a result of its opposition to the War of 1812 was a lesson every practicing politician knew. Soon after the Civil War began, the Republican
New York *Times* was drawing the analogy, for the benefit of
the state's Democratic party, between the "peace party of
1814–15, and the peace party of 1861."[9] By contrast, the example of the Mexican War of 1846–1848 was not often recalled in
the Civil War. Parties had carried on as before throughout
that conflict, and indeed the Civil War president had then

been an outspoken critic of the war—but it was a foreign war and the United States did not suffer invasion or rebellion during it.

The fall of Fort Sumter brought all American politicians face to face with a real rebellion, and assertions that parties were suddenly irrelevant to the national life abounded. President Lincoln was too canny to make such statements once the war began, but one of his private secretaries, John Hay, did acknowledge the common assumption in January 1862, referring to the "professions of leading Republicans, that former party politics are to be ignored in this great struggle for the National Life."[10] Lincoln tended to be fatalistic and likely knew it was too much to expect that the Democratic party would agreeably disappear until he could bring the war to a successful close.

Other politicians loudly espoused the no-party assumption at war's outbreak. Opposition leader Stephen A. Douglas rushed to pledge fealty to the Union and to denounce partisanship after the fall of Fort Sumter. "There are but two parties," he said, "the party of patriots and the party of traitors. [Democrats] belong to the first." That rare example of lofty eloquence from the practical Douglas would often be quoted during the war. Even the difficult New York Democrat Fernando Wood, who would soon become a symbol for partisan obstructionism or worse, vowed at first, "I know no party now."[11]

Renouncing party feeling was easy when there were no major elections in sight and Congress was not in session, as was the case in April 1861. Most northerners likely assumed the war would end in the summer, after a show of force or one battle shocked the rebels into submission. Vague ideals of a partyless nation did not face a nationwide test of sincerity or intensity in 1861, and many people believed the crisis would all be over before the full slate of off-year elections came in 1862 anyhow.

Nonpartisanship was, at least for a time, a reality in many parts of the country. *Wilkes' Spirit of the Times,* an independent and nonpolitical sporting newspaper published in New York City, observed on April 27, 1861, "All political divisions have disappeared in the face of the humiliation with which the country was menaced."[12] Unsystematic statements of the no-party assumption abounded, especially in Republican news-papers and in war rallies called without respect to party. "We have done with partizanship as long as this war continues," insisted the ardently Republican Chicago *Tribune* late in the summer of 1861. And at a great war meeting at Bryan Hall in Chicago on Saturday night, August 24, 1861, the participants adopted a resolution "that all political parties ceased to exist and were merged into one common organization for public defence, when treason first lifted its . . . head."[13] The nonpar-tisan ideal was itself susceptible to partisan manipulation, of course. Pennsylvania in 1861 offered a full menu of exploita-tion of the theme for party gain.[14] In counties where Repub-lican dominance was overwhelming, the Democrats in des-peration urged sharing offices according to a no-party ideal for the war. Republicans in such areas clung to party labels self-righteously. Where the Democrats were more competi-tive, they spurned the customary Republican appeals to ig-nore party. Thus, in Allegheny County, whose seat was the growing metropolis of Pittsburgh, Democrats, who had seen a total of 16,725 votes cast for Lincoln in 1860 as against 7,818 for his opposition, sought a union of parties for upcoming elections. In Berks, on the other hand, the banner Demo-cratic county of the Keystone State, where Lincoln polled only 6,709 of 16,111 votes cast in 1860, the Democrats opposed abandoning party organization for the upcoming elections.[15] And Democrats in York County, where the Republicans in 1860 had been outvoted 6,633 to 5,128, did not bat an eye in maintaining their organization steadily. York's Democrats professed to believe that the no-party idea had originated with Republicans, whereas the Allegheny County Democrats pointed to Stephen A. Douglas as the father of the idea and repeated his admonitions against party in their Pittsburgh paper for months.[16] Recognizing the pattern of self-interest, the Pittsburgh Republicans complained that "the Democratic game is a shrewd one to again get in the ascendancy in our State. They go straight Democratic tickets in Democratic counties, but in Republican counties they demand a one-sided kind of Union wherein the Republicans are asked to abandon their organization while the Democrats preserve theirs in full force."[17] By the time the season to prepare for the 1862 elections arrived, however, Pittsburgh's Democrats were meeting in county and state conventions as usual. And the no-party ideal was renounced for partisan organization by June. They blamed the Republicans for refusing to honor non-partisan arrangements and for changing the goals of the war from saving the Union as it was to emancipation.[18]

It was generally a more attractive ideal to Republicans, already in control of the national government and most state governments, than to the Democrats or other parties remaining from 1860, but the ideal proved at least convenient for the New York *World,* a newspaper of weak party identification before its financial takeover by convinced Democrat Samuel L. M. Barlow in August 1862. The *World* would become the banner Democratic newspaper in the country, but in May 1862 its editors disapproved of movements to organize parties for the fall elections as "premature"—despite the fact that New York faced a gubernatorial contest as well as elections for members of Congress and the state assembly. Movements for opposition organization, the editors said, looked "to the continuance of the war long after the period when the war will probably be over." "We believe," the editors stated flatly, "that political parties must arise on the close of the war, but we deprecate any attempt to revive the Democratic organization. The questions with which that party is historically identified have become obsolete."[19]

At the end of June 1862 the *World* roundly condemned the organization of an opposition political party:

> All movements looking to the early creation of an opposition party are ill-judged and mischievous. Every man with any just pretensions to sagacity must see that the organization of such a party would comfort and encourage the rebels and strengthen them abroad . . . No one who knows anything of the nature of party warfare can doubt that the embittered feelings engendered by mutual recriminations, would in a short time lead such a party to obstruct the administration in every practicable way, and to do all in its power to bring the conduct of the war, and consequently the war itself, into discredit. It must be remembered that the administration of President Lincoln has nearly three years to run, and that no opposition party, unless it accomplishes a revolution and overthrows the government, can put the reins into new hands until long after the period

> when, with reasonable support, Mr. Lincoln will
> have brought the war to a close.[20]

July 1862 proved a crucial time, because General George B. McClellan's grand effort to capture Richmond in the Peninsular Campaign failed, making the prospect of continued war certain. And all states faced elections in that year.

Taking New York as an example, we find vivid evidence of the reaction to the failure of McClellan's campaign. The first day after the bad news arrived, Republicans reported the city as experiencing once again a "war surge." It was as though the "old experiences of the Sumter and Bull Run epochs" were repeated in aroused feelings of patriotism on the streets. The next day, the old pro-southern wing of the Democratic party in the city, led by Fernando Wood and James Brooks, staged a mass meeting at the Cooper Institute. Its resolutions still professed to lay "aside all prejudices and attachments, whether of party or locality," and vowed its support for General McClellan, who retained command of the Army of the Potomac despite his defeat. But the discontented Democrats expressed sentiments against emancipation of the slaves and insisted that "this is a Government of white men, and was established exclusively for the white race."[21]

The Democratic State Executive Committee met in Albany in July, and by September the *World,* which now clearly represented the less disaffected wing of the Democratic party in New York, reversed course and condoned party organization. In autumn its editors supplied systematic and rational arguments for an opposition party, effectively answering their own previous assertions and failing, of course, to acknowledge their earlier contrary position on the question.[22] The editors had embraced the arguments out of convenience, but they articulated well themes that were readily available.

The canvass started late, and the New York election was little discussed in the papers until the end of September, attention having been diverted by the continuing military campaign in Virginia, culminating in the second disastrous defeat at Bull Run at the end of August and the subsequent alarming invasion of the North by Robert E. Lee's army. Politicians of both parties naturally watched with bated breath to see the outcome before committing their organizations to positions on the issues of the war.

In other words, the pattern for political parties in New York City was clear. One opposition party faction proved more eager than the other to place engaging issues before the people, but all politicians, facing the likelihood of news of momentous military events, preferred to await the outcome before taking stands on issues before the people. Even if elections were pending, they would wait extraordinarily late to get the news and make the canvass briefer than usual. But when election day arrived, they would be organized.

OTHER POLITICIANS and political activists expressed sincere no-party views in private. The famous New England orator and intellectual Edward Everett, who ran for vice president of the United States on the Constitutional Union ticket in 1860, provides an interesting example. When in the late summer of 1861 he was solicited by another Constitutional Union party leader in Massachusetts to participate in meetings to choose candidates for elections, Everett responded:

> Without having heard the pros & cons, I would say that in my judgment nothing is to be gained, at this time, by separate party action. We have no separate issue to go upon. We go with the entire North, for the vigorous prosecution of the war . . .
>
> It is true the Republicans have not, thus far, pursued a magnanimous course. They have monopolized all the civil offices, & have conceded to their opponents only the opportunity, in some cases, of taking the risks of military life. This is human nature. I do not council abstinence from separate party action, as a matter either of justice or generosity toward our opponents, but of justice to ourselves as good citizens & good patriots.
>
> Let them have the offices & let us do our duty.[23]

Another candid example comes from the opposite coast, in a letter C. A. Reed, a member of the Oregon state legislature, wrote to Illinois Republican Senator Lyman Trumbull on June 17, 1862. Oregon Senator Edward D. Baker, a Republican, had been killed in action at the Battle of Ball's Bluff, and the legislature was on the eve of electing a replacement. Reed explained:

> Our State Legislature (of which I am a member) meets the second Monday in Sept next. It will there be our duty to elect a U.S. Senator to fill the vacancy caused by the death of the lamented Col Baker . . . What I desire of you is information whether it would be better for the interest of Ore-

gon & the United States to elect to that office a
man who is a Republican or a Democrat both being good union men—Your knowledge of matters
at Washington will enable you to give me the desired information. I believe the Republicans will
have the power to elect a Republican Senator if
they think proper, having the majority in both
houses. Yet many of us desire to do that which
will result to the best interest of the country regardless of former party ties. Your immediate answer to this will be thankfully received . . . I voted
for the election of our present President and still
believe I done right, yet the spontaneous uprising
of all parties in defense of the government blots
out in a measure past party issues.[24]

Public affirmations of no-party sentiment became a staple
in the political discourse of War Democrats.[25] As for the Republicans, confronted with the reality of party competition
in mid-1862, some denounced it, others faced it with philosophic resignation, and still others fell simply into old habits
of meeting competition with competition and no comment.
Republicans, however, seldom affirmed the two-party ideal
during the war. One exception came in the New York *Evening
Post*. In the gloomy late summer of 1862, after the second defeat at Bull Run and with Democratic opposition looming at
the polls, the editors of the *Evening Post* bitterly blamed the
administration for the revival of the Democrats and accepted the "necessity" of party competition:

Those who believed that party government must
cease during the war did not, we think, appreciate
all the conditions necessary to a healthful and

vigorous conduct of the government. Parties have
wrangled in England during all the great wars,
and the necessity of parties has become daily
more evident for some months past. We are not,
therefore, either surprised or alarmed at the reap-
pearance of the democratic party as a party; we
believe that its vigorous opposition may yet stir
the Administration to such wise and active measures as will enable it to save the country.[26]

The position of the *Evening Post* in this instance was out of
step with the Republican party in the state, which attacked
the Democrats and their popular gubernatorial candidate,
Horatio Seymour, in large part because the Democrats had
chosen to mount an opposition. Sincerity was thereafter
hard to judge. Seymour's address to his nominating convention had thrown down the gauntlet, declaring the necessity
of organizing an opposition, and the Republicans had taken
up the challenge with a will. The principal speaker for the
Republicans and Unionists in this important campaign
was not their gubernatorial nominee—a wealthy general
with antislavery credentials, James Wadsworth, who presumably was supposed to be on military campaign—but the ex-
Democrat and candidate for lieutenant governor, Lyman
Tremain. Tremain took steady aim at Seymour's assertions
of the "supposed benefits of party organizations," arguments which Tremain maintained had "little force in a crisis
like the present." On the contrary, Tremain said, "Jefferson
Davis rejoices to see the formation of these parties."[27]
In the shortened but intense fall campaign in New York—
watched with much interest by politicians all over the country—Republicans performed a delicate dance. They implied,

with statements like Tremain's on Jefferson Davis, that the Democratic organization in fact aided the enemy, but they made sport of the Democrats when they expressed outrage at being called traitors. Republicans maintained that they did not call the Democrats traitors—as indeed Tremain had not done directly in his Jefferson Davis statement.[28]

It is difficult to take seriously the allegations made on either side in this important early political campaign of the Civil War. The Republican gambit, ignoring state issues and implying treason to the nation but stopping short of forthright accusation, seems too measured to represent sincere shock at the spectacle of organized opposition. Likewise, the Democratic expressions of wounded feelings seem calculated for effect—nineteenth-century politicians were used to the roughest of accusations in every canvass.

And yet, in their tentative and near-bantering way, the New York politicians were playing with fire. Some eager politicians might decide to ride the treason hobbyhorse to electoral victory, and some people might well take the charges seriously.[29] By 1863, as the next chapter will show with chilling evidence, many in fact did take them seriously, and some of those people were armed.

POLITICIANS' STATEMENTS made in an election campaign must always be treated with some skepticism, but nineteenth-century politicians did not trifle with the patronage, for it provided the basis of their party organization. The subject has been little studied in recent years but in this instance proves revealing.[30] When Abraham Lincoln assumed the presidency in 1861, he brought his new political party to national power and national offices for the first time. Lincoln and the Republicans were partisan products of the American party system in the era before civil service reform, and they intended to operate as their predecessors and opponents had done. Of course, they did not intend to imitate the Democrats in gaining a reputation for corruption, but they did intend to fill most civil offices with deserving Republicans who in 1860 had worked for party victory at the polls.[31]

Historians who have given the question any thought have assumed that the Republicans did precisely that; talk of a "clean sweep" is common.[32] The leading authorities on the subject, Reinhard Luthin and Harry J. Carman, stated that after the election of 1860 "the change in party control . . . was the occasion for the most sweeping removal of federal officeholders up to that time in American history," and they pointed to the removal of 1,195 of 1,520 presidential officeholders. Carl Russell Fish, on whose earlier work Carman and Luthin relied, spoke of "the completeness of the overturn in 1861."[33] Fish had enumerated 1,457 removals from 1,639 places. Fish also noted that 362 recess appointments in the Treasury Department were made for new offices created by the Civil War tax legislation and did not actually represent removals. Luthin and Carman evidently subtracted that number, 362, from the overall total, 1,457, to arrive at their figure for Lincoln's total removals: 1,195. But they made a subtraction error—their figure should have been 1,095.[34]

The New York Custom House might well be considered the center of this intense party activity, and Carman and Luthin quoted a New York *Herald* article from the Civil War estimating that some 1,200 jobs were at stake there alone.[35] That figure is also erroneous. Every job in the custom house was listed, with its occupant's name and salary, every two years in the government's *Official Register.* In 1861 there were but 785 jobs in the custom house. Republican tariff legislation during the war necessitated an increase in the work force, but there were still only 1,027 jobs in the custom house in 1863.[36]

The notorious reputation of the pre-civil service reform parties far exceeded their actual performance in the Civil War. Based on a name-by-name comparison of New York Custom House officeholders listed in the *Official Register* for 1859, 1861, and 1863, only 53 percent of Democratic officeholders from 1859 had departed by September 30, 1863.[37] In fact, the figure attributable to political removals is much lower. The turnover in the custom house was rapid even at times when presidential administrations were not changing. Between 1861 and 1863 the collector, the head of the custom house, turned out 42.6 percent, many his own appointees. If all of these were removals for cause rather than politics, then the new Republican collector of the port, Hiram Barney, a favorite of Secretary of the Treasury Salmon P. Chase, in his first five months of direction may have replaced as few as 10.4 percent of officeholders for political reasons alone. And those might have been, given the extreme pro-southern conservatism of New York City's Democratic party (symbolized in the prominence of Fernando Wood), the southern sympathizers among the Democratic holdovers.

Hiram Barney's restraint seems anomalous only if we believe that assumptions about the usefulness of political parties did not change with the advent of war. But they did change, even in that red-hot cauldron of party discipline the New York Custom House. Barney's letters, piecemeal, reveal what happened. Pennsylvania Republican Senator David Wilmot, for example, wrote him a couple of weeks after the fall of Fort Sumter to complain that his patronage demands had not been met: "You gave me encouragement to hope you would allow me to supply the places in the Custom House now held by F. A. Ward of Susquehanna Co. and Olmstead of this Co. . . . It is but right that these changes should be made." At the bottom of Wilmot's demanding letter Barney noted: "Answered May 2/61 Saying I could not now do what I intended to do when we anticipated no war & no need of democratic cooperation & declined his request."[38]

Complaints poured in from Republicans less idealistic than Barney. The King's County Republican central committee, for example, passed resolutions in September 1861 calling for Barney's removal from office because of "weakness and unsound political action, in the delays attending his appointments of Republicans to office." Later that month other Brooklyn Republicans called a meeting to protest the resolutions that had condemned Barney. The counterresolutions described the earlier King's County committee meeting as "thinly attended," and these less office-hungry Republicans professed their "full confidence in the *capacity* and *integrity of the Honorable Collector* and in his desire to satisfy without needless delay all just claims upon him for office *under the present condition of the Country.*"[39]

It did not take long for the tone of exasperation to become threatening among Republicans accustomed to peacetime levels of partisanship. In an anonymous letter denouncing the treasonous sentiments of various custom house holdovers from "the late infamous Administration," a man who signed his letter "One Who Knows" asked, "How long Mr Collector is this suicidal system to be pursued or tolerated? Unfortunately, the same game was played by the Whigs, until they were 'played out.'"[40] Jersey City Republicans complained in June 1861 that "the refusal thus far to make any appointments within the districts named, has produced marked dissatisfaction, and threatens to be disastrous to our Republican organization. While there may be force and propriety in the position taken by you and others exercising the appointing power to refrain for the present from making a *general* change, based upon political sentiment, yet in our judgment, it is best, if not absolutely necessary, to make a few removals and new appointments."[41]

The collector seems to have felt that he was following administration policy. Twenty-first ward politician Thomas Van Buren wrote Barney in May 1861, "Since you intimated to me some weeks since that the policy of the Administration which you intended to follow, forbid changes in the Custom House to any extent, I have not troubled you with any applications."[42] Whatever the policy's origins, Barney was set on adhering to it. S. C. Johnson spoke of the collector's "determination to make no more appointments in connection with the Custom House, except for cause, other than party, at present."[43] Democrats noticed his unwonted generosity; one mentioned in the late summer of 1861 "the liberal course you have so far pursued."[44] Republicans, in turn, naturally resented the favored Democrats. When rumors of fraud in the custom house circulated, one unhappy Republican asked sarcastically, "Is it true that they are the work of *patriotic* Democrats retained in place of our own men?"[45] A few Republican officeholders shared the collector's generally unpopular position. The superintendent of police in New York, J. A. Kennedy, for example, told Barney, "Although I am not of opinion that this is the time to make any changes in the official force under you, yet when the time may come," and then added his recommendation for office.[46]

But on the whole, Barney's behavior proved unfathomable

to spoilsmen. An associate of the collector's corrupt assistant A. M. Palmer reported having seen the collector once or twice in Washington, D.C., "but he is as mysterious here as in New York—a man whose ways are past finding out! He will go out of office as he came in, an enigma to many, but none will assail his integrity or purpose or fidelity to the government."[47] In the end Palmer's corruption—aiding the evasion of the blockade, which got him arrested by military authorities and thrown into Fort Lafayette in 1864—began Barney's undoing. The steady stream of complaints about his appointing philosophy helped gain him a reputation for being unable to control his own shop, and by summer the Seward-Weed faction in New York capitalized on anti-Chase sentiment, on Barney's lack of popularity among Republican wire-pullers, on distrust of him by merchants because Barney was a lawyer, and on the pressures of a perilous-looking presidential canvass to force him out.

When Lincoln considered replacing Barney in 1864—a momentous action in a presidential election summer—he first solicited opinions from politicians and organizers in New York. Most seemed to agree that Barney should be removed, and all who did seemed to agree on the reason—ineffectual political judgment. An operative named James Kelly put it most vividly: "I was in our Central Committee with him three years where I never knew him to offer a suggestion, support or oppose a Resolution, in fact all must admit that he is a perfect negative man, and possesses no knowledge of politics in any shape, and makes no pretentions to such knowledge. When first appointed he stated it was war times and men should not be removed for their political opinions [and] . . . such balderdash, yet we were constantly hearing of entire strangers receiving lucrative situations."[48]

John A. Gray, who told Postmaster General Montgomery Blair of the need for a Republican leader in New York for the approaching election, agreed in substance. "Barney," Gray said, "is a good fellow—my personal friend—but totally unfitted for his post. He is purely a negative character—Honest & inoffensive." His "heart" was not in politics.[49] Disillusion was Barney's lot. "If I have been unable to satisfy politicians," he said, "I can only say the thing is impossible— Besides that, the Custom House in New York can never be well conducted as a business establishment while it is run as a political machine."[50]

Application of the nonpartisan ideal during the war was piecemeal and not guided by edicts handed down from the president or the cabinet. In other words, the policy in the New York Custom House turned out to be Hiram Barney's policy. In Boston, by contrast, at least 81.5 percent of 1859 officeholders were removed from the Republican administration by 1863, and in Philadelphia slightly more than 90 percent.[51] Treasury Secretary Salmon P. Chase affected a high-minded approach to patronage, but he let the collectors set their own policies, on the whole.[52]

WHEN HISTORIANS DESCRIBE the resilience of the "party imperative" in the Civil War era, they tend to think of it in terms of electoral competition or congressional voting rather than in terms of patronage or pelf. But the partisan imperative also manifested itself in the ability of the organizations' anonymous workers and placemen to resist the idealism of some of the party's leaders.[53] The New York Custom House in the Civil War reveals that darker side of the persistence of party. Idealism came from the top down—in the Treasury Department, from Chase and his apostle Barney. From the bottom up came a culture of corruption.

The custom house in New York was a wonderful place to work—"a place which no one ever leaves voluntarily," observed one commentator—if one did not want to work hard. It was a frustrating environment if one wanted to accomplish anything worthwhile. In the first place, it did not work. Barney simply could not get the job done—collecting tariff duties efficiently—with political appointees and without a merit system. After shocking discoveries of corruption were made in 1863, but before the final disaster of Palmer's arrest, Barney told President Lincoln that he regretted "most deeply these disgraceful transactions," and he said that he was "mortified" at having "reposed confidence in unworthy persons." "But," he added, "it is impossible to avoid some mistakes of this character so long as the government offices are filled in the manner they are & subject to political influences as they must be to a considerable extent."[54] In the second place, corruption was endemic no matter what party was in office. Third—a point made discernible during the war—patriotism was rarely a consideration of anyone working at the custom house or hoping to work there. From today's corporations we hear much talk about the "culture" of particular workplaces, and the custom house by analogy definitely had its culture: of selfishness, sloth, and corruption.

Work could not be performed efficiently because ultimately the institution was not aimed at work; it was aimed at abetting party organization. The business hours explain much: 9 to 3.[55] Clerks frequently complained that their desks were overburdened and that they regularly took work home with them.[56] Little wonder, for their six-hour day did not afford enough time to collect the nation's customs duties expeditiously at the busiest port in the country during the biggest war in the nation's history. At election season, moreover, many employees worked on politics, not on tariffs.

Invariably the workers in the custom house said that other departments did not work hard. The workers themselves recognized the culture of loafing, though they always pointed to other loafers than themselves. Weighers, for example, were notorious for not standing by their scales during office hours. And even when there was weighing to be done, they left it to their assistants. Sinecures were common.

Letters of recommendation for jobs in the custom house sometimes betrayed the writer's knowledge of how the system really worked. When William Cullen Bryant recommended retention on the custom house rolls of Joshua L. Pell, he began by saying that Pell was "no drone" and ended by pointing out that Pell had worked hard in the past "at periods when the New York Custom House was full of idlers and rogues."[57] When Amasa J. Parker recommended retention of a man in the bonded warehouse, he was at pains to say that the man had "none of the vices or indolence that sometimes belong to modern office holders."[58]

The workers' short hours and slack discipline stemmed ultimately from the operation's political organization. Hope of promotion was stunted as a motivator. The lowly placeholders and organizers could rise to a certain level in the party, but they did not really dream of becoming the chief executive or one of the powerful men who chose the chief executive because these were rarely promoted from within. The powerful men were the candidates for and holders of elective office. The workers got out votes and organized parades and rallies in return for rewards of salaried offices. The custom house was not the main stairway to the presidency, the governorship, or the Congress.[59]

The placemen expected the system to operate in war or peace. The collector and his boss, the secretary of the treasury, had the preservation of the nation high on their agendas. In the custom house, the job—that is, the salary—was perhaps as important as anything. To such underlings, the office of collector of the New York Custom House was, as one Frank W. Ballard put it, "second, in importance and influence, only to the Presidency itself."[60] Surely anyone who could make such a statement lived in a subculture where officeholding was divorced entirely from policy and statesmanship.

Proof that the greater political purposes of the nation did not loom large in the custom house lies in the fact that there was no policy to make military service an official consideration in hiring for the New York Custom House. Service records were rarely mentioned by applicants or by men making recommendations for office. One man, Luke Gore, even stated in his letter seeking a job for his 23-year-old son that it would help him to avoid the draft.[61] Among the many applicants' letters surviving in the papers of the collector during the Civil War, only five mentioned military service. The most inspiring came from a radical newspaper editor from upstate New York, Ambrose H. Cole, who stated that he would not ask for a job did he not have a "withered limb" which kept him from "fighting the battles" of his country.[62] Another applicant who had joined the army after being turned down for a job at the custom house earlier and had been wounded, applied again, and Barney noted that he ought to have a place.[63] One applicant pleaded hardship because he had five sons in the army and three daughters and a boy still at home.[64] And T. Bailey Myers recommended his son and pointed out that he had been rejected for military service.[65] Louis Ruttkay applied for a position in the naval office at the custom house and noted that although he was not "personally in the army," he had "a brother there and without being drafted . . . furnished a three years' substitute last summer."[66] Pale patriotism sufficed.

On the whole, it is not the record that is remarkable but what is absent from the record: in letter after letter about places in the custom house during the war military service is not mentioned. That would have been impossible in the population-strapped Confederacy. There, acute manpower shortages caused congressmen and newspaper reporters to hound the government bureaus in Richmond to prove that they were not havens for draft dodgers. Government departments repeatedly described their clerks, making sure that the public understood that they were disabled or overaged men with large families to support. Even the Confederate Secret Service was staffed by invalids and men with disabling injuries or conditions.[67]

The failure to link patriotism and patronage, unlike the early nonpartisan appointment philosophy of Barney, was administration-wide. It was not until July 1863 that Lincoln began to think about the problem, and it took a startling coincidence to bring that about. Lincoln finally told the postmaster general:

> Yesterday little endorsements of mine went to
> you in two cases of Post-Masterships sought for
> widows whose husbands have fallen in the battles
> of this war. These cases occurring on the same

day, brought me to reflect more attentively than I had before done, as to what is fairly due from us here, in the dispensing of patronage, towards the men who, by fighting our battles, bear the chief burthen of saving our country. My conclusion is that, other claims and qualifications being equal, they have the better right; and this is especially applicable to the disabled soldier, and the deceased soldier's family.[68]

This letter to Montgomery Blair was not exactly an order: it did not say that in the future post office appointments must favor veterans and their families, all other qualifications being equal. Nor is there any evidence that the policy was immediately applied to all government departments. It apparently never applied to the Treasury Department.[69]

The press took up the cause in a desultory way. The high-minded New York *Evening Post,* for example, editorialized about the many disabled soldiers in northern society in July 1863, saying that "such places as those of postmasters, assessors and collectors of internal revenues and their assistants and custom-house clerks, can be well filled by our disabled veterans."[70] Later that year Congress passed resolutions in support of giving the preference to disabled and discharged soldiers in filling jobs in the departments.[71]

Putting self before country, however, lay at the heart of the custom house culture—and, critics had always said, lay at the heart of political party organization. The people who thought parties illegitimate thought of them as operating from the opposite of patriotic motives. That there was selfishness and greed in the operation of political parties is undeniable.[72] It is easiest to glimpse the culture in the manuscript records of an internal Treasury Department investigation of the New York Custom House conducted in the winter of 1862–1863.[73]

Of all the workers called for interrogation, not a single one prefaced his testimony with a statement of the mission of the customs service, its importance to the revenues of the United States government, and its critical role in raising money for the Union war effort. Not a one spoke of dedication to service to the mercantile community of New York or to the Treasury Department. The workers were imbued with no sense of mission, with no ethic of craftsmanship or competence, with no code of service to public or country. The most honorable of the lot stated that they did their jobs, refusing money offered by merchants and their agents to expedite attention and taking the customers' business in the order it came to them.

Many admitted accepting emoluments beyond their salaries from importers and their agents. These ranged from routine Christmas gifts presented to workers by clients to free shopping sprees for custom house clerks in importers' stores and hundreds of dollars accepted in cash annually.

THE WORK OF THE New York Custom House stands as a reminder that we should not let our observation that the two-party system survived the Civil War tend too much to the celebratory.[74] For the mid-nineteenth-century two-party system was as unregulated and raw as the industrial system of the Gilded Age and perhaps equally unsuited to the demands of the twentieth and twenty-first centuries. The Republican and Democratic parties of Lincoln's era operated in freewheeling style, unhindered by civil service reform, ballot reform, effective voter registration laws, and a host of political adjustments that separate our era from theirs.

The persistence of the two-party system during the war was as much a work of the anonymous as the famous, but for the ordinary clerks and poll workers on election day, the men who painted banners and built floats for parades, the organization's nameless stalwarts, its placemen, and, for want of a better term, hacks, the two-party system had nothing in particular to do with the war effort. The persistence of the two-party system during the Civil War was the persistence of an unreformed system, the political analogue of American capitalism before Progressivism, let alone the New Deal. It was a matter of business as usual, and some of that business definitely put self before country and party before public safety.

2

"Blustering treason in every assembly"

THE REVOLT AGAINST POLITICS IN 1863

THOUGH MANY HAD DOUBTS about the utility of political parties in times of rebellion or invasion, hardly any American questioned the role of elections during the Civil War—or any of the other general outlines of the polity prescribed by the Constitution of 1787. Unlike the two-party system, the basic constitutional parameters of the republic had been substantially internalized by the middle of the nineteenth century.

It is all too easy to overlook the framing role played by the Constitution in the Civil War. Because the conflict was a rebellion and a civil war precipitated by secession, we have tended to think of the Constitution as problematic in this period rather than "configurative." The great constitutional historian James G. Randall entitled his definitive book on the subject *Constitutional Problems under Lincoln,* and yet the problematic parts of the Constitution were few, the habeas corpus clause most notably. In my own previous work on the Constitution in the Civil War, I too focused on the problematic parts. But it pays handsome dividends to think, as a new generation of constitutional historians led by Arthur Bestor and Harold M. Hyman did, of the problems the Constitution solved for the Republicans and Lincoln.[1] In fact, this new way of thinking has not been carried far enough. Just as it shaped and channeled the arguments over slavery in the antebellum period, some of the provisions of the Constitution shaped the war and channeled the national energies. The much-venerated document's provisions, silently molding the grand political outlines of the American republican experiment, were seldom consciously articulated at the time, but they may therefore prove all the more important. For Americans had so internalized the shape the Constitution gave to their peaceful republic that it never occurred to them to question the ways in which it would shape the republic at war.[2]

A bicameral legislature, congressional power over the purse, civilian control of the military, and other basic provisions of the Constitution went unquestioned. For the political parties, though of course they were unmentioned in the Constitution and largely uncontemplated by its drafters, Article I, section 2, which established terms for members of the House of Representatives at two years, was the most important clause for the Civil War. It meant that if the war lasted as long as two years—and the failure of the Peninsular Campaign on July 1, 1862, guaranteed that it would—the country would have to hold major national elections during wartime.

As the historian Roy F. Nichols observed many years ago, the timing of American elections throughout the nineteenth century served to maintain political interest at a fever pitch.[3] This was as true of the Civil War period as of the antebellum era, which witnessed a notorious heating up of the sectional controversy.

The inexorability of the American electoral process marks one of the most important differences between the American political system and parliamentary systems. As Nichols put it, "In the United States the recurrence of elections is relentless. By constitutional prescription political contests must take place at stated intervals, regardless of the condition of public affairs. The calendar rather than the need of the moment summons voters to the polls."[4] Even in time of war, Nichols might have added, Americans have presidential elections and—every two years—congressional elections, as well as state elections and many others not mandated by the United States Constitution but by the numerous state constitutions that resemble it.

In the Civil War, elections not only marched irrepressibly to their own calendar, but the states had arranged the dates to suit their needs in the peaceful prewar period, as no national bodies exerted systematic control of the election processes. The result was a calendar liberally sprinkled with important election days, from the spring in New England to late summer and autumn further west and south. Only the presidential election was held at the same time in all states.[5] The chart on page 38, adapted from the political Bible of the nineteenth century, Horace Greeley's *Tribune Almanac and Political Register*, lays out the complicated calendar of elections for the country in 1862. Even in a politically fallow year like 1861, a few elections of importance were scheduled. The New England states elected governors and state legislatures, while New York City chose a mayor and New York State elected important officials below the level of governor. Seven other states held gubernatorial elections, and four chose members of the next United States Congress a year earlier than most states. Pennsylvania held elections for the state legislature and other local offices and, as circumstance had it, Illinois chose delegates to a convention to revise their state constitution.

ELECTION SCHEDULE IN 1862

California	First Thursday in September.
Connecticut	First Monday in April
Delaware	Second Tuesday in November
Illinois	First Tuesday in November
Indiana	Second Tuesday in October
Iowa	Second Tuesday in November
Kansas	Second Tuesday in November
Kentucky	First Monday in August
Maine	Second Monday in September
Maryland	First Wednesday in November
Massachusetts	First Tuesday in November
Michigan	First Tuesday in November
Minnesota	Second Tuesday in November
Missouri	First Monday in August
New Hampshire	Second Tuesday in March
New Jersey	First Tuesday in November
New York	First Tuesday in November
Ohio	Second Tuesday in October
Oregon	First Monday in June
Pennsylvania	Second Tuesday in October
Rhode Island	First Wednesday in April
Vermont	First Tuesday in September
Wisconsin	First Thursday in November[1]

Source: *The Tribune Almanac and Political Register for 1862* (New York: Tribune Co., 1862), p. xxx.

The year 1862 was more important politically, of course, with most of the off-year congressional elections as well as many state elections to be held. But every year saw important elections. In fact, the Civil War lasted forty-eight months, and in at least half of those months major elections occurred in the North. On average, then, the North witnessed a major election every other month of the war.

In the summer and autumn of 1862 it dawned upon both Republicans and Democrats, surprised alike to see the war lasting so long, that elections would operate as usual. The politicians generally obeyed old habits and organized for the inexorable election calendar prescribed by the Constitution. These elections made Republicans nervous. Not a single Republican, however, questioned holding the elections. The constitutionally prescribed elections were internalized for Republicans and Democrats alike, but the organization of opposition parties to contest the elections in the midst of a rebellion did not enjoy the same explicit constitutional mandate. Elections were internalized, but the role of parties, in wartime at least, was not. And therein lay the fundamental political problem of the North during the Civil War. There would be elections, certainly, but whether to condone the organization of parties to contest them was at best uncertain. Thus there was a tinge of envy in northern denunciations of the southern "despotism" they claimed to face in the war. The New York *Evening Post,* for example, in 1862 explained the astonishing stubbornness of Confederate resistance in part by pointing to the advantages of despotism in war. The Confederacy, the editors said, had "no divided Congress to embarrass the action of her Executive . . . She allows no divisions among her people, no factious mass meetings to distract public opinion."[6]

Some Republicans, even among experienced politicians, seemed surprised that the Democrats were organizing for elections. As seasoned a political veteran as Illinois Senator Lyman Trumbull felt called upon to warn the president:

> The Democrats are organizing for a party contest this fall They have called a state convention and are calling congressional and county conventions of a purely party character throughout the State. The party in Ill. as you must be aware from their course in the constitutional convention last winter is under the control of leaders who sympathize with the South & if they get control of the State, Ill. which has done so much and so nobly for the Union in this struggle, will be paralyzed, if her influence is not thrown positively against the government. This must not be, & to thwart it a counter organization is a necessity.[7]

In ordinary times of peace, the Illinois Democrats' actions in organizing for the elections—holding state conventions and the like—would have occasioned no surprise, of course.

In state elections in New York, Indiana, Ohio, Pennsylvania, and Illinois in the fall, Democrats enjoyed greater success than expected, apparently because of voters' dissatisfaction with Union military defeats. When Democrats assumed their hard-won government positions in January 1863 and pressed opposition policies in state governments, particularly in the Illinois legislature, about which Trumbull had expressed fears before the elections, many in the country were genuinely shocked—none more so than the soldiers in Illinois regiments stationed in the South.

A TYPICAL POLITICAL RALLY in Illinois reveals popular expectations about the role of political parties at a time of rebellion. On Saturday afternoon, February 21, 1863, farmers in western Illinois flocked to an Unconditional Union War Meeting in Macomb. Under the circumstances, the meeting was well attended. It snowed, and to make matters worse, the frozen crust on the roads was not hard enough in some places to bear a horse, so some of the farmers had to walk as many as five or six miles to attend the meeting. Sixty men chartered a railroad car and traveled from tiny Prairie City, some twenty miles away. The rally required booking the largest room in Macomb, which was located in the Methodist Church.

The agenda for the meeting was typical of the era. Political rallies often lasted all afternoon and well into the night, whatever the weather. The organizers drew up and adopted resolutions, and while the resolutions committee met, the choir sang songs like "Then We'll Rally 'Round the Flag, Boys." Later, they sang "The Star Spangled Banner," and two local politicians spoke before dinner; another spoke after dinner.

First up on the platform in the afternoon was George C. Bates, who, as the Chicago *Tribune* reported his speech, "compared the North with the South, as to their unity of sentiment." Bates pointed to the advantages in the political unity of the Confederacy. "There [in the South] they entertain but one idea, which is to secure their independence, as a separate Confederacy. There you hear nothing of political parties or cliques—all are united for the accomplishment of one object . . . Our misfortune here in the North is that we still cling to old party names and party preferences . . . The more intelligent and honest men of all parties have broken party shackles and staked their all upon the altar of the Union." He then proposed, according to the *Tribune*, "that political platforms be entirely laid aside till after the war was over, and all party names and dictates and dogmas of political parties thrown aside." Bates ended by reading from George Washington's "Farewell Address"—it was the day before the anniversary of Washington's birthday—with its famous denunciation of party spirit as dangerous to republics.

The advent of Democratic majorities to the Illinois and Indiana legislatures as a result of the autumn elections came as quite a shock to Republicans, some of whom had thought that the opposition might not even organize to contest elections. Democrats, energized by their local victories, wasted little time in getting up resolutions and initiating bills that angered excitable Republicans and seemed to threaten the war effort. The actions of the Democrats in the two states were similar and smacked of a concerted party strategy that transcended state boundaries. Resolutions called for an armistice and a convention of commissioners from the states to meet in Kentucky to negotiate peace. Laws were drafted to shift control of the state militias from the executive to boards created by the legislatures.[8]

The most remarkable result of the shock of having the Democratic opposition actually assume power in familiar legislative halls was the near-revolt of the Illinois line. The movement started on January 30, 1863, and lasted until April 22, 1863. The first regiments to react to news of the Democrats' maneuvers in the Illinois state legislature were stationed in Corinth, Mississippi. On January 30 the officers and men of the 7th, 9th, 12th, 50th, and 52nd Illinois Infantry denounced "the bitter partisan spirit that is becoming dangerously vindictive and malicious in our state," rejected any notion of compromise or armistice with the Confederacy to end the war, and stated flatly: "Should the loathsome treason of the madmen who are trying to wrest from [Governor Richard Yates] . . . a fraction of his just authority render it necessary in his opinion for us to return and crush out Treason there, we will promptly obey a proper order to do so."[9] Despite the drastic and threatening nature of the resolutions, there were but ten dissenting votes among the thousands of soldiers assembled by their officers to hear and vote on the resolutions. The soldiers' meaning was clear: they threatened to turn about-face, march to Illinois, and drive the Democrats out of the state legislature if the Republican governor gave them the order to do so.

On February 13, regiments at Bolivar, Tennessee, declared that they "came to this war from all parties, but know only one party now, that which is vowed to save the Union," and promised, "Should treason rear its monstrous form at home . . . we will only wait for the first base act of treason, to turn back and crush" it.[10] The next day, the 82nd Illinois Infantry, stationed near Stafford Court House, Virginia, drafted a series of resolutions and expressed their regret that they were "no longer at Camp Butler [outside Springfield, Illinois], to have an opportunity of liberating the halls of our capitol, from this detestable scum."[11]

On March 5, the 39th Illinois Infantry, stationed at Port Royal, South Carolina, professed themselves "unalterably opposed to raising party issues in Congress, in State Legislatures, or elsewhere at the present time, and in our opinion, he who attempts it, is a traitor to his country." They swore "to oppose and put down traitors wherever found, whether in the cotton-fields of the South, or in the wheat-fields of the North." On March 14, the 56th Illinois, camped near Helena, Arkansas, unanimously declared it "the duty of every citizen to lay aside all party creeds, platforms and organizations and stand firmly by the powers that be."[12] From Warrenton, Missouri, came the resolutions of the men of Merrill's Horse, 1,200 strong, who agreed unanimously "That . . . should any of our fellow citizens differ in political views with the present Executive, in his administration of our national affairs, it is the imperative duty of all to lay aside such party issues for the present, as we in the army have done."[13] On April 2, the 88th Illinois Infantry, stationed near Glasgow, Kentucky, with but two men dissenting, asked Illinoisans at home to "lay aside all petty jealousies and party animosities" and declared: "We hold ourselves ready to obey an order from the President to march into our State with bayonets fixed to enforce the laws."[14]

I have discovered resolutions from 55 Illinois infantry regiments, 4 cavalry regiments, and 4 batteries of artillery, altogether representing perhaps some 50,000 men.[15] That equals the size of a Civil War army. The resolutions varied in content, but all denounced compromise and armistice with the Confederacy, nearly all denounced continuance of political party conflict, and many contained threats against legislators at home. Resolutions from at least 22 of the regiments and 2 of the batteries, representing upward of 20,000 men, contained threats to return to Springfield if . . . if the governor or the president gave them the order, if the Democrats persisted in their treason, if duty made it necessary.

Almost all of the resolutions were threatening—and, taken as a whole, downright chilling. I know of no similar threats from large numbers of organized military forces against civil power in all of United States history. The resolutions, the first concerted political voice heard from the army during the war, did not sound the music of moderation. The resumption of normal party activity in the Illinois legislature nearly provoked an armed revolution among the Illinois soldiery.

Opportunity for political agitation among the soldiers lay in the curiously leisurely pace of the Civil War. War then was still essentially pastoral and seasonal. The war's rhythms by twentieth-century standards were slow and sometimes verged on the ritual. In the winters, the armies ceased campaigning by tacit mutual agreement and hibernated until spring or early summer weather permitted men to march, wheeled vehicles to roll along dirt roads, and draft animals to graze on new pastures. It is notorious, for example, that the Army of the Cumberland went into winter quarters on January 1, 1863, right after the Battle of Stone's River, and remained there until the end of June—six solid months of inaction.[16] Even as relentless a campaigner as Ulysses S. Grant entered winter quarters as a matter of unthinking routine in 1864-1865, despite mild criticism from the northern press.[17]

The political result of the armies' custom of going into winter quarters has never heretofore been noticed. In winter the Civil War armies, composed mostly of voters and newspaper readers, sat in tents and snug log huts with little to do but talk about politics. These were citizen volunteer armies, on the whole, with men only temporarily removed from mainstream political society and, even more important, led by men who in private life had been, many of them, politicians and civic leaders.[18]

Thus, in the early months of 1863 idle Illinois soldiers for the first time saw the results of a breakdown in a moratorium on party politics that had been imposed by the distracted politicians themselves. The soldiers had not reacted to the autumn elections of 1862 because the soldiers were busy fighting—up to the December battles of Fredericksburg in the East and Stone's River in the West. The Illinois legislative session opened on January 5, 1863, with the Democrats in control. And just as some Illinois troops for the first time in months could sit down by the fire in winter quarters and read the newspapers from home, they read of partisan opposition to Republican measures related to the war in their home state.[19]

The soldiers' resolutions did not often reach to Republican-controlled states, except as a spillover from the Illinois regiments, here and there, though some regiments from all states were entering winter quarters. And not all Democratically controlled states faced substantial criticism from their soldiers. New York and New Jersey, with Democratic governors, for example, did not find their soldiers arrayed against them in resolutions threatening political violence.

Though the reaction varied from place to place and was most extreme always in the states of the Old Northwest, the principal explanation lies in the reality of opposition; an opposition party that truly threatened to control the government was, it turned out, intolerable to many Americans in wartime.[20] The abrupt end of the near-revolt is easily explained: by late April military campaigns had resumed on many fronts, so the soldiers were too preoccupied by marching and fighting to focus on politics back home. Anyway, back home, the Illinois legislature had recessed in February, and when it came back in June, the Republican governor managed to get it dissolved on a constitutional technicality.

The Democrats were left speechless by the soldiers' resolutions—another remarkable and unparalleled fact. Their newspapers mustered little response. The resolutions—threatening a coup d'état rather than warning against one—lay well outside the rules of the political game as usually played. They may have struck genuine fear in the hearts of Democrats. Whatever the case, the Democratic press regarded them as somehow unanswerable.

Only the most partisan of organs came up with a challenge. The York, Pennsylvania, *Gazette,* for example, was elevated in journalistic stature only a little above a political party bulletin board,[21] but unlike the big metropolitan Democratic newspapers, the *Gazette* responded. The newspaper printed at least three critical letters purportedly from Pennsylvania soldiers in the field but anonymous and without regimental identification. One of the letters maintained that officers threatened anyone who opposed the resolutions with being put in the front rank in the next battle. Another said that officers called only for ayes but not for nays, and still another maintained that no one voiced opposition in his unit because of fear of arrest for mutiny.[22]

And Clement L. Vallandigham answered them as well. In a speech in New York in early March, he maintained that officers, eager for the perpetuation of the war and their comfortable salaries, saw to the adoption of the resolutions "concocted in Indianapolis, Columbus, Springfield, and Washington city, and sent down to be clothed with the form of an expression of the regiments, but really an expression of the opinion of the officers alone." No man would be deterred at home from free speech by their threats, the Ohio Democrat said defiantly.[23]

THREATENING REVOLT against politics was not confined to simple soldiers and their officers but reached eastern intellectuals and the urban social elite. Francis Lieber's widely circulated pamphlet *No Party Now but All for Our Country* was published not in the presidential election year of 1864 and not at the time of New York's hotly contested gubernatorial election of 1862. Instead, it was published in 1863 and represented a reaction, like that of the Illinois soldiers, to the reality of political opposition. Lieber first presented it as a speech before a meeting of the Loyal National League in New York City on April 11, 1863, and it was published quickly thereafter.[24]

In fact the Union League movement and the Loyal Publication movements themselves constituted a part of this revolt against politics. When Henry W. Bellows came to New York to dedicate the Union League Club building there in the spring of 1863, he described the origins of the movement in harrowing terms. He began his speech with scenes of bitter civil war: a sixteen-year-old boy who witnessed his mother's murder, counted the nine wounds in her body, and then enlisted in the Union army; a Union man, threatened with being shot through his parlor window by five brothers-in-law, who set out to kill them all and had so far got three of them. These were incidents from Missouri, and Bellows said: "It was the possibility of scenes like this in our own communities that started the Loyal Leagues. In Baltimore, where they began, the danger was not merely imminent . . . The invasion of Pennsylvania aroused Philadelphia to a sense of her own peril as a possible border city . . . New York . . . did not know, from party appearances and animosities, how soon it might become necessary here to compel every man openly to show his hand. There was blustering treason in every assembly."[25]

These organizations and their "propaganda" literature did not have their origins in Republican tactics for an election season, and thus remind us once again that the anti-party movement, though convenient for Republicans, was not always cynical. The true origins of such organizations, attitudes, and literature lay in the shock and disbelief that political opposition could arise at such a crisis.

For their part, the Democrats apparently found the Union Leagues as threatening and novel as the Illinois soldiers had found Democratic opposition in legislatures of the Old Northwest. After the presidential election of 1864, the New York *World* attempted to reconcile Democrats to the unfavorable result, but the editors could not swallow the Union Leagues' role in the campaign. "Their bigoted agency," said the *World*, "is the only part of the late remarkable presidential contest in which we find it difficult to forget the animosities of party strife now that the election is over." The Democrats felt it necessary, in the case of the Union Leagues, to "protest against a kind of warfare so alien to the spirit of the age and the genius of our institutions." The *World* referred to "espionage," to "political intolerance," and to "organized social exclusion" that seemed intended "to crush free thought and enforce a degrading uniformity of opinion."[26] And yet the Union Leagues appear from a modern perspective merely to have fueled the customary techniques of party warfare with the monetary resources of the wealthy classes of modern cities. Neither Democrats nor Republicans were well prepared for serious party opposition in the midst of rebellion.

WHERE POLITICS carried on as usual during the war, the unusual still threatened. In January 1863, for example, the Pennsylvania state legislature convened in the wake of the 1862 elections to select a United States senator. Joint ballots to choose senators became the principal focus of attention in state governments at the beginning of a legislative session in senate election years, and Pennsylvania politicians had been calculating for the event ever since the final count from the autumn elections came in. When the politicians added up the results to see what the composition of the legislature would be, they discovered that there was one more Democrat than Republican.

At that point the eyes of many Republicans in Pennsylvania turned to Simon Cameron. It may seem odd. After all, Cameron's career lay in what many would regard as discredited ruin. In 1861 he had gone off to Washington to run the War Department, but he had proved unequal to the demands so great a war placed on so unprepared a country and lasted only ten months in the office. Moreover, in the confusion resulting from mobilization, Cameron found his reputation tarnished with irregularities if not outright corruption in organizing men and materiel for war. This shadow darkened his already shady reputation. He left the cabinet to become diplomatic representative to the Russian court at St. Petersburg—a nineteenth-century equivalent of banishment to political Siberia.

The question remains, why would eyes turn to such a person at such a critical time in Pennsylvania politics? The answer, put plainly, is that when there was a one-vote margin against the party in the legislature, some in the party turned to the man who could likely buy that vote. Cameron's notorious reputation included previous attempts to gain the Senate despite his party's being in a minority in the legislature. In 1845 Cameron, then a Democrat, had won a senate seat with the support of Whigs against the nominee of the majority Democratic caucus.[27] In 1857, against a Democratic majority in the state legislature, Cameron emerged as a Republican U.S. Senator amidst widespread charges of bribery.[28]

The Senate was within tantalizing reach again in 1863. Pennsylvania held its elections in October, and before the end of October 1862 one Republican from Milton, Pennsylvania, told Cameron, "We have *one* of a Democratic majority on joint ballot in the Legislature, and it is presumed by many that if you were the candidate for the *U.S. Senate,* you could control that vote."[29] Less than three weeks later, another wrote him to say, "I believe you are the *only* man we can elect U.S. Senator . . . I told some of my Democratic friends you would be on hand again and that you were sure to beat their majority of one. They said no, they had got clear of all the shaky Democrats . . . and Cameron could not play the old game of forty five, in sixty three."[30]

Even Cameron's friends came close to admitting his "special" qualification for this particular senate race. Benjamin H. Brewster, for example, wrote from Philadelphia to dissuade Cameron from running for the Senate so that he could run for governor instead. Brewster pointed out that Cameron could not gain the senatorial election without the imputation of fraud because the Republicans were in a minority.[31]

Surprisingly, Cameron's surviving papers reveal, in some instances, what was offered and to whom. From Philadelphia early in December Cameron learned of one likely prospect, the member-elect from Perry County, a man named John McGee, the editor of a newspaper called the Perry *Democrat*. Cameron's informant, a man appropriately named Wiley, had learned from the incumbent Republican that McGee "could be induced to vote for you for U.S. Senator. He says he knows him to be anxious to make something:—is poor, and has had a rough time getting along."[32]

The McGee scheme apparently did not work out, but another Republican operative had a different idea, one that could work only during the war. He suggested that William L. Alexander, editor of the Clarion *Democrat* and a member-elect also, "is clearly guilty of discouraging enlistments, and we desire to know the moment when to have him safely removed to Fort Lafayette or some other safe place."[33] Perhaps reliance on military arrest of a civilian who was also an opposition newspaper editor and elected officeholder proved too much even for the desperate politicians of Pennsylvania, and this scheme was not attempted either; but the hint of using methods other than political was a harbinger of developments to come in the tight Pennsylvania contest.

In the end, hopes came to focus on a man named Nelson and on another named T. Jefferson Boyer. C. S. Minor, a Cameron operative, described what Nelson was offered: a government contract for his father and an appointment for life for himself. As for Boyer, papers in that case do not survive in the same collection, but Cameron's able modern biographer, Erwin Stanley Bradley, relied on evidence presented in a later legislative investigation for proof that Boyer was offered a $20,000 bribe. All the schemes eventually failed, and Cameron's bid went down with them: Democrat Charles Buckalew became Pennsylvania's U.S. Senator.[34]

Cameron's schemes did not fail because the Democrats were incorruptible. They failed because the Democratic party in Pennsylvania created tremendous disincentives for bolting to Cameron on the joint ballot. The most important disincentive was threat of assassination.

Rumors that the Democrats might hold their members to party regularity by armed force circulated well before the joint ballot, because the Democrats knew perfectly well why the Republicans were turning to Cameron as their candidate. As early as November 1, 1862, one of Cameron's political allies wrote Cameron's son, "Tom McDowell was here recently & I understand says any democrat who will vote for your father will be assassinated." He dismissed the threats as "gammon," but others took them more seriously.[35] Another Cameron supporter warned the candidate himself from Harrisburg that same month,

> I have it from what I at least consider a good reliable source that there is on foot a conspiracy to defeat your election to the US Senate by the next Legislature at all hazzards. It has been stated to me confidentially that Alderman [Bill] McMullin . . . was at the head of 1000 desperate characters at Philadelphia who were to come to Harrisburg during the election of U.S. Senator, station themselves in different portions of the Hall of the House of Representatives, and that they were to shoot the first democratic member or Senator who should vote for you, that several Republican members were also to be assassinated.[36]

Not a thousand but some number of armed men did station themselves in the legislature on the day of the joint ballot, and the result caused great alarm among Republicans. The Democrats naturally held firm on the vote, and Cameron lost his bid. The unusual circumstances provided Republicans with a face-saving excuse afterward for having lost the election. One disappointed supporter said that the election "show[s] the sober thinking class that the cause of Democracy is desperate, when they must resort to threat and fire arms to carry out their designs."[37] But another Cameron man was more inclined toward serious retaliation. He wrote in great anger and indignation afterward, "Without a display of mob force your election was certain . . . It was a great mistake, that the Govr did not have out the military to protect the Legislature—Such a display would have secured a fair election—I am well satisfied, that we are yielding too much to rebel sympathizers & their mob allies—We need force—despotic force by the Government to put down treason at home . . . we should have controlled the late elections by force if no other way."[38] Harrisburg came closer to civil war than it might look on the surface. Cameron, for his part, apparently had contacted U.S. Marshal William Millward in Philadelphia and was surprised when federal forces did not appear in the assembly on the day of the vote.[39]

The Pennsylvania Senate election could be said to illustrate the persistent vigor of the two-party system during the Civil War. Because senators were not popularly elected and candidates often surfaced only after the popular elections for the state legislatures and sometimes only in the legislatures at the time of the joint ballots, the intrigues were as issueless as any great political strife in the American party system; there was no need for platform statements or slogans. Indeed, no issues of war and peace or civil liberties and treason or race and slavery played a visible role in the Cameron-Buckalew contest. These deliberations were truly the arenas of intrigue and faction by the power-hungry that their critics said they were.

But the persistence of such purely political contests in the midst of a great war resulted in strange distortions of the two-party system. For even the issueless intrigue of Simon Cameron and the attempt of the opposition Democrats to enforce serious party discipline on their own somehow came to be perceived as related to wartime issues—hence the strident postmortems on the senate race by the disappointed Republicans quoted above. Persistence of normal political practices—when those practices included desperate brinksmanship and when the assumptions of the culture at large made politics out of place under the circumstance of rebellion—resulted in nearly uncontainable extremes of behavior and of rhetoric.

In other words, the normal operation of politics in state capitals like Harrisburg, Pennsylvania, or Springfield, Illinois, could be mistaken for conspiracy and sedition at a time when politics was supposed to be suspended for the national good. And violent and constitution-wracking solutions to disputes over office lay readier to hand—hence the idea of having the military arrest a Democrat who had criticized the draft in his newspaper.

BEGINNING WITH the reorganization of the Democratic party for the elections of 1862, the North was replete with accusations of conspiracy. To be sure, allegations that the opposition party was conspiring against the republic were themselves politics as usual in mid-nineteenth-century America. The fledgling Republican party had rallied its voters against the dreaded "Slave Power Conspiracy" in the 1850s. And the Republicans in turn had to fend off a major challenge from the American party, which rallied its hosts against an imagined papal plot directed at Protestant America. For their part, the southern secessionists had gained a vital popular following by warning voters against a "Black Republican" conspiracy to enslave white southerners in an unconstitutional republic.

But there were two marked differences from politics as usual during the Civil War. One lay in the near possibility of violent result. Thus, Republican Governor Oliver P. Morton of Indiana apparently misperceived the first stirrings of Democratic organization for the fall elections in 1862 as the beginnings of sedition. In June 1862 he wrote the secretary of war to warn him that "a secret political organization" had arisen in Indiana. It numbered "ten thousand strong," and one of its objects was "to circulate and foster news papers of extremely doubtful loyalty." Morton then named long-operating Democratic newspapers like the *Indiana State Sentinel*, the Cincinnati *Enquirer*, the Dayton *Empire*, and the Chicago *Times*. Professions of loyalty from such sources were but a disguise, he insisted, and he pointed excitedly to articles published in the papers casting doubt on the constitutionality of the recently passed Legal Tender Act. The traditional images of subversion abounded in Morton's letter. The enemy was everywhere—"confined to no particular locality"—and they were "bound by oaths and their meetings . . . guarded by armed men." He asked the War Department for "at least 10,000 stand of good arms" which he would put in the hands of "our loyal citizens to be organized as militia throughout the State, under the law creating the 'Indiana

Legion.'" The governor unashamedly sent a copy of his alarmist letter to the president as well.[40]

Say what one will about the plausibility of Morton's letter, it was not written for popular political effect. He sent it to men who were, like him, seasoned veterans of politics. They likely knew that the newspapers he mentioned were old Democratic organs. Yet they were also officials in positions to make civil war possible—the president and the secretary of war really controlled such resources as 10,000 good rifles and really could dispatch them to Indiana.

We can glimpse a similarly dangerous excitement in Illinois a little later—at the time of the Illinois soldiers' resolutions against the resumption of politics. After the Democrats gained a majority in the state legislature, the administration of Republican Governor Richard Yates requested the dispatch of federal troops to Springfield under the guise of recruiting, but actually to watch the legislature. Political competition again went ominously farther than peacetime confrontations. Yates and other Republican officeholders in Illinois wanted the federal troops placed "under the Command of some loyal commander who may be clothed with military power to declare the State under martial law if need be; and disperse the legislature."[41] Yates managed to dissolve the legislature constitutionally in June, but an unpopular draft call later that summer found the Illinois governor still convinced of "a settled purpose of revolution in the State," complaining that Illinois was still defenseless, and asking for a greater number of troops than in his previous request.[42]

But by the middle of 1863, not all politicians were easily transported back to the conspiratorial frame of mind of the 1850s and before. Too much water had flowed over the political dam in decades of fierce party competition in the United States. For all the charges of conspiracy that were thrown around, political parties had maintained a constant presence in the republic for a long time by the 1860s. Thus, Richard Yates's requests were not acceded to by the administration, and neither were Morton's. Some politicians, like the president, proved generally skeptical about such allegations.

And these differences in judgment bring to mind the second difference between the conspiracy charges of the 1850s and those of the Civil War—a difference that points to the central problem of interpretation of Civil War politics. As the political historian Michael F. Holt has pointed out, the success of a political movement built around allegations of conspiracy against the republic lay ultimately in being able to point to a pattern of real events that made the party's allegations of conspiracy credible and powerful to anxious voters. Thus, the phenomenal rise of the American or Know Nothing party in the middle of the 1850s raised American Protestants' anxieties about Roman Catholicism to crisis pitch because of a fortuitous pattern of actual events. The new immigration of Irish Catholics and Germans in the late 1840s, the trusteeship controversy within the Catholic Church in America, controversies over Bible reading in the public schools, and the visit of a papal nuncio named Gaetano Bedini lent plausibility enough to prejudiced Protestant voters.[43]

Likewise, the successful organization of the Republican party at the same time fed off "Bleeding Kansas," the caning of Charles Sumner on the floor of the United States Senate, and the United States Supreme Court's Dred Scott decision.[44] Naturally, these same Republicans, when faced with opposition at the polls in the Civil War, chose often to campaign in the familiar "paranoid style."[45] The slave power was gone from the United States government, but Republicans found a new monster to slay: sedition in the North. It worked well enough, apparently. But the problem from our modern perspective is that the pattern of real events requisite to make the new allegations plausible has always seemed weak. Where are the sensational equivalents of the events of the 1850s during the Civil War?

They are suspiciously and mysteriously missing. And that fact has led baffled historians to improbable conclusions about Civil War politics. An entirely cynical interpretation concludes that the Republican accusations were consciously counterfeit smears of a loyal and long-suffering opposition. Yet such interpretations have never had great following because of the problem of such letters as Oliver P. Morton's about the threat in Indiana. Why address such a letter to a savvy Republican like Lincoln instead of to the anxious voters in Indianapolis? It seems as though men like Morton might have believed what they said.

The more persuasive conclusion has been to diminish the importance of the conspiracy charges, to push them to the background of political controversy in the Civil War, and to regard them as high jinks rather than allegations of high treason. In the most influential piece of writing on Civil War politics ever published, the historian Eric L. McKitrick ruminated on the problem and essentially brushed it aside:

> Something might be said about the functions of
> an opposition which is under constant suspicion
> of being only partly loyal. The Northern Demo-
> cratic party during the Civil War stood in pre-
> cisely this relation to the Union war effort, and

its function in this case was of a double nature. On the one hand, its legitimacy as a quasi-formal institution would remain in the last analysis unchallenged, so long as it kept its antiwar wing within some sort of bounds. But by the same token there was the rough and ready principle that "every Democrat may not be a traitor, but every traitor is a Democrat."

Thus, the very existence of the Democratic party provided the authorities . . . with a ready-made device for making the first rough approximation in the identification of actual disloyalty. It also provided a kind of built-in guarantee against irrevocable personal damage should the guess turn out to be wrong. When in doubt they could always round up the local Democrats, as many a time they did, and in case of error there was always a formula for saving face all around: it was "just politics." There was, in short, a kind of middle way, an intermediate standard that had its lighter side and alleviated such extremes in security policy as, on the one hand, the paralysis and frustration of doing nothing, and, on the other hand, the perversions of power that accompany political blood-baths.[46]

But there was no such "formula." I spent almost a decade studying the military arrest of civilians in the North during the Civil War; and in compiling the records of some 14,000 victims of arrest, I found not a single case in which the arresting authorities performed their work in any spirit except grim dedication and determination. I never read the case of a prisoner of state, languishing in Fort Lafayette or Old Capitol Prison or some other "bastille" in the North, who did not regard his plight as serious in the extreme. An interpretation of the internal security issue in Civil War politics as "just politics" having "a lighter side" has simply lost touch with the feel of contemporary reality during the Civil War. It has imposed its own ironic but comfortable familiarity with the workings of political parties in twentieth-century America back into a period that could feel no ironic distance on party competition and felt more than uncomfortable with party competition in the midst of a great war.

It nevertheless remains true that Republican crusades against the Great Northwest Conspiracy, the Knights of the Golden Circle, the Sons of Liberty, or other alleged grand fifth-column movements against the Union lack plausibility. In hindsight, their targets were feeble, vague, and even seriocomic organizations.[47] How then are we to make sense of Civil War politics?

It is crucial to keep in mind the context of beliefs about the role of political parties in times of invasion or rebellion described in Chapter 1. With many Americans believing that parties had no proper role at such times, allegations of conspiracy did not require so compelling a pattern of actual events as in peacetime. Political organization itself became a threatening event.

3

"He must be entrenching"

POLITICAL PARTIES AND THE DEATH OF STRATEGY

THE FIRST YEAR OF THE WAR witnessed an unusual phenomenon: focus by the American press on something *other* than politics. The timing of the American Civil War, its outbreak only about a month into a new presidential term, with as few important elections on the year's calendar as was possible in the politically contentious republic, left the partisan press with fewer party controversies than usual to discuss and offered instead a different subject of admittedly grave importance demanding attention. The loose moratorium on party competition felt necessary by some politicians likewise dampened the editors' customary appetite for political blood. And there was no denying that the war was a sensational subject ripe for journalistic exploitation.

The popular press covered the Civil War closely, and that coverage is a hallmark of the war's celebrated modernity.[1] "The modern American journalist emerged for the first time in the Civil War," a recent study of the "Bohemian brigade" tells us, and such associations of modernity with detailed coverage of military operations by the popular press are common, if somewhat vaguely explained.[2]

Under close examination, however, northern press coverage of the war hardly seems precocious. Because the press itself was not really modern in form or outlook but was in fact a pre-professional institution dominated by the two-party system, it could not and did not have a "modernizing" effect on the war.[3] The northern press failed even to detect and describe the war's modern aspects.

In the middle of the nineteenth century there really was no journalism; there was only politics. As the historian of journalism Michael Schudson has remarked recently, the press at that time was a branch of politics.[4] Or, as a disillusioned newspaperman in the late 1850s expressed it, "No party could exist for a year without it . . . It is the ordnance department of politics, the arsenal and magazine from which small minds draw their weapons and ammunition for political warfare."[5] Newspapers usually took money directly from a political party or were kept financially afloat by government advertising from the party in power or by pressure exerted by the party out of power on its members to subscribe to the newspaper.[6] Of some 1,600 newspapers published in the North at the beginning of the Civil War, 80 percent were "political in their character," according to the United States Census of 1860; and making allowance for the religious and agricultural press, one could say the newspapers were with only a few rare exceptions political.[7]

Newspapers existed not to report the news but to promote one party and to denigrate the others. News was so incidental to their craft that most newspapers, operating in small towns and villages across the country, employed no reporters—only editors to scribble editorials and pressmen to set type. They clipped the news indifferently from the great metropolitan dailies and went themselves about the serious work of promoting their party and abusing the opposition in editorials on the inside pages.[8]

The lack of professionalism was apparent to many, including journalists themselves. It evinced itself before the war in occasional complaints about "party organs" and their editors the "organ-grinders,"[9] but a most revealing incident occurred in 1864. The New York *Tribune* suggested "A Novel Notion," the establishment of schools of journalism. When the editors of the Harrisburg *Telegraph* heard about the proposal, they dismissed it with derision, equating it with "the necessity of lying being taught as a branch of the fine arts."[10]

WAR OFFERED opportunity to the press but posed a problem. The mid-century press had no war correspondents. Lacking expertise in observing war and lacking true professionalism, reporters hired for the purpose fell back on their store of general knowledge about the nature of fighting. In other words, they brought to the interpretation of the war the values of the culture at large. We get a good idea what these beliefs were from a scene on the eve of the first large battle of the war, the Battle of Bull Run, when a reporter ran into Charles Sumner of Massachusetts emerging from an animated informal discussion with others on the floor of the United States Senate. "Senator Sumner, his face lighted with pleasure, came to tell me the good news," said the reporter. "'McDowell has carried Bull Run without firing a shot. Seven regiments attacked it at the point of the bayonet, and the enemy immediately fled.'"[11] The rumor was false, of course, but the conversation, which occurred on July 20, 1861, on the eve of the battle, reveals the military expectations of the culture: easy victory gained by attack with the bayonet.

American reporters flocked to the Bull Run battlefield the next day, along with the famous London *Times* correspondent William Howard Russell, who had covered wars on other continents before. The employment histories of the Americans who wrote the earliest lengthy accounts of the battle are instructive: one, Edmund Clarence Stedman, was thrown out of Yale and became a small-town editor and sentimental poet; another, George Wilkes, was a former pornographer turned editor of a paper that covered horse-racing and boxing.[12] Stedman recalled in later life that the "early correspondents, of whom I was one, knew nothing of military life, tactics, modern warfare."[13]

It is not surprising to find such ideas as Senator Sumner's voiced before the great battles of the Civil War, but it is surprising to find them reiterated throughout the war. In fact, they did persist, and, if anything, escalated in importance.[14] The explanation of that anomalous fact lies with the press as much as anywhere.

Proof that there were no American military experts or war correspondents to comment on the action lay in the fact that, even though American reporters swarmed to the Bull Run battlefield, they and their readers waited to "hear what Mr. Russell will say."[15] Russell, who had gained considerable fame for his coverage of the War in the Crimea five years earlier, seared onto the northern memory an unbearably humiliating image of pell-mell flight from the Confederates. Determining the lessons of the Bull Run defeat became a major preoccupation for American newspapermen over the fallow political year.

The consensus of the Republican press after Bull Run was that the army needed professional leadership; organization, training, and discipline; confidence to ignore the premature urging to action the politicians and the press itself; and patience.[16] In other words, the army needed George B. McClellan, whose secrecy, contempt for the president and War Department, obsession with organization, and postponement of attack would become the exaggerated perversions of the military lessons of Bull Run. McClellan did not turn out well, but reasons for the failure of his generalship lay in the very circumstances of his appointment to command.

Other values emerged from analysis of the defeat as well.[17] What seemed required to expunge the humiliation of Bull Run did not point the country in the direction of the modern tactics and strategy of World War I. On the contrary, many of the lessons pointed decidedly backward. The New York *Times,* for example, reported a little over a week after the battle, "The enemy are very reluctant to meet on the open field; they do not seem to like cold steel, and fight like Indians under cover . . . On a fair field, Southern guile will soon give way to Northern sturdy valor." "A battle," the *Times* maintained, was "like a prize-fight" and demanded "the utmost possible concentration of bodily strength within a given time." In such "ring struggles," the editors said, "it is well known the 'trainers' never allow drinking of water—only moistening the mouth."[18] So in the hot Virginia sun the answer for the army, presumably, was less and not more water.

Such were the dysfunctional results of turning the nimble political wits of the editors to a subject other than politics.

Within three days of the battle, the New York *Evening Post* had likewise convinced itself that the battle had been an unfair fight against superior odds and an entrenched foe. The paper reassured its readers "that in any fair, open, hand-to-hand fight, the Union troops are too much for the seceders."[19] The future held mainly "A Chance for Heroes."[20] The New York *Tribune* also insisted, "We can beat the Rebels with equal numbers on even ground" and expressed confidence that the North would eventually "compel them to come out of their skulking places and meet the Unionists in the open field."[21] Because McClellan stated in an early interview that the war would be determined by artillery, newspapers also published several articles about Parrott rifled cannon—manufactured in New York—but the emphasis in the New York press lay with visions of individual heroism, the use of the bayonet, and attacks in open fields.[22]

High-brow criticism was equally enslaved to these popular values. In an influential article on Bull Run published in the *Atlantic Monthly,* Charles Eliot Norton sought to explain the "Advantages of Defeat." "Though the science of war has in modern times changed the relations and the duties of men on the battlefield from what they were in the old days of knighthood," he wrote, "yet there is still room for the display of stainless valor and manful virtue." Norton, a man of letters and descendant of an old New England elite family, knew nothing of war, but that was true of the press corps as well, and both interpreted the Civil War in terms of chivalry.[23]

The sports writer George Wilkes proved surprisingly

influential. *Wilkes' Spirit of the Times,* published in New York City, was a "gentleman's" weekly, covering the turf, field sports, and the stage, but the war aroused a patriotic spirit in Wilkes, who could not at first resist the lure of military service and left the city immediately to join up. In the end, he remained a civilian but accompanied a New York regiment on the Bull Run Campaign and sent dispatches home regularly.[24]

He proved as romantic as any journalist covering the war. Wilkes particularly admired the exotic uniforms of the Zouave regiments, with their billowing red pantaloons, blue jackets, and red caps. After several days in camp, he concluded that the war would be settled not by marksmanship but by the bayonet. He theorized that war had evolved from the spear to gunpowder and back to the spear again, in the form of a bayonet on the end of a rifle. "I will merely point to the fact," he wrote knowledgeably, "that the Government has already taken away the little costly breech-loading toys which the munificence of New York put in the hands of Col. Ellsworth's regiment, and served out to them the spear, in the shape of a sabre on the end of a Minie musket . . . The sabre bayonet is also to be distributed throughout the entire army, and I feel certain, from what I have gathered through military men, that the actual embrace of battle, man to man, is what the Northern captains of this war intend mostly to rely upon."[25]

"There was not a bayonet charge made by the National infantry during the day," "Bull Run" Russell lamented in a follow-up dispatch about the battle. And how the northern press longed for the day when the Army of the Potomac would answer the insulting reproach of the British observer. Yet, the reporters soon learned that military hospitals treated few blade wounds. In May 1862 the *Evening Post,* for example, reported about the Battle of Shiloh that although it was *apparently* a hard-fought battle, there was, according to the army surgeons, only one bayonet wound treated in the hospitals. The editors could only conclude that, whereas it was true that bayonets rarely actually crossed on the battlefield, "The mere appearance of an impetuous and determined bayonet charge is generally counted upon as decisive by commanders. The troops charged upon are almost sure to seek shelter from the dreadful sight."[26]

In such judgments, Americans of the Civil War era revealed the gulf that separated them from our modern age. When war reporters learned that blade wounds were rare, they were apt to conclude either that the battles had not been fought hard enough or that the assaults were so impressive that the enemy fled before the bayonets could reach them. Today's historians are apt to reach a different conclusion: that the absence of blade wounds was an indication that the bayonet was a useless and retrograde weapon of the romantic past, on its way to the military trash heap along with bows and lances. But thinking in the latter modern fashion will keep us from entering the mindset of the Civil War.

In the political lull of 1861–1862, the pre-modern press froze the Civil War in the heroic language and amateur values of combat derived from European and aristocratic cultures of which, ironically, the country's press and politicians were otherwise critical. When the journalists left their accustomed realm of politics, they were literally at a loss for words—and borrowed them from available cultural sources, however alien. Their coverage of the war had no particular modernizing effect because the press was not imbued with modern values regarding war. On the contrary, the reporters and editorialists made the war look antique. Their language and values for military analysis came from the age of chivalry.[27]

Indeed the press brought to the war a medieval understanding of combat, with its images of the duel, the spear, the open field, the test of physical heroism—the way war was decided, as the great military historian John Keegan says, *before* the gunpowder revolution, let alone the Minie cartridge and the rifled musket.[28] Whatever the realities of the battlefield, in the realm of press coverage the Civil War was not in any meaningful sense the first modern war.

Amateur "war correspondents" brought these values to the American perception of the war and then more or less left them there. With the return of vital political party activity in the autumn of 1862, newspapers shifted their attention to familiar questions of politics rather than to learning about the technology of modern warfare. Press and politicians alike applied these frozen assumptions to analysis of McClellan's failure on the Peninsula of Virginia in mid-summer 1862. Because the Democratic party emerged, ready to compete, at the same time that George B. McClellan suffered defeat on the Peninsula, Republicans always had difficulty ignoring partisanship in assessing the reasons for the astounding defeat, which traumatized northern public opinion. Criticism of strategy and tactics in the Civil War was rarely free from partisan bias after the summer of 1862.

It was clear before McClellan's failure what he stood for. As the Republican Chicago *Tribune* expressed it near the time of his appointment to command the Army of the Potomac,

"The misfortune at Manassas has given to the army a young, vigorous and scientific General."[29] It was also well known that McClellan was a Democrat. An unfortunate consequence of the concatenation of events in the summer of 1862 was that military science—symbolized by the headline-dominating McClellan and summed up in the term "strategy"—often became an object of partisan denigration. Even so, these somewhat confused and distorting ideas would likely have died with the dismissal of McClellan from command in November had he not emerged early as the likely Democratic candidate for president in 1864.

George Wilkes led the way in criticizing McClellan in a series of articles that appeared in late summer of 1862. The most influential of his articles, published August 4 and widely reprinted in other newspapers, questioned McClellan's loyalty, alleging he had a past affiliation with Cuba schemes and filibusters to expand slave territory and was enamored of the South. It rooted the general's "bloodless strategy" in a political desire to coax the rebels to a convention to reconstruct the Union and not to drive them to a "battle à l'outrance."[30] Southern sympathies "emasculated [McClellan] of a great portion of that vigor and devil which is the first requirement of a fighting general."[31]

Wilkes helped establish the narrative from which McClellan's military reputation never recovered. On the Battle of Yorktown, for example, the sporting journalist said, "Instead of taking the meagre city by assault, and giving the North and East an opportunity to square accounts of glory with the West, his bloodless strategy was again put in play, and he distributed the shovel instead of drawing . . . the sword." After the Seven Days' battles, too, Wilkes alleged, McClellan would "relinquish the musket for the spade."[32]

Wilkes also accused McClellan of making it a practice to arrive on the field of battle only when the fighting was over, and he contrasted that behavior with the general's bombastic dispatches. "During all the while," wrote Wilkes, "he went riding up and down the lines, assuring 'the boys' that if they would 'stick by him, he would stick by them,' and occasionally telling them, in the imperial vein, to have no fear, for he would expose his sacred person, with them, in the dangers of the field." Yet at the Battle of Malvern Hill, the general could be found "high up in the rigging of the [gunboat] Galena, with a spy-glass in his hand surveying the turmoil on the shore."[33] Wilkes added an image of disease by faulting McClellan for his choice of field of battle, the swamps of the Chickahominy, where "the siege of Yorktown" became "truly only the siege of death and disease against the . . . army" with its "damp trenches" where Union soldiers were "saturated into death with fatal fevers."[34] The articles were published in pamphlet form in 1863 as *McClellan: From Ball's Bluff to Antietam* and gained notoriety in part from Wilkes's lack of close partisan identification.

Partisans soon took over the debate. The Republican radical newspaperman Van Buren Denslow, from Yonkers, New York, for example, offered for the 1862 election campaign a pamphlet, based on a series of his newspaper articles, entitled *Fremont and McClellan: Their Political and Military Careers Reviewed.*[35] Denslow constructed a heroic system for evaluating generalship in which fighting came to be contrasted favorably with "strategy."[36] For example, he criticized Union high command for rejecting General James Shields for promotion. They had done so, he charged, because, "being a fighting general, [he] was voted rash and no strategist." "Success," Denslow concluded, "depends not so much upon knowledge as upon those qualities which command knowledge, and without which all knowledge is unavailing, viz.: character, energy, and will." Summing up McClellan's failure on the Peninsula, the editor saw "in all this disaster that mysterious phantom 'strategy.'"[37]

Denslow tended to think in conventional images of sabers and bayonets when he considered "fighting" as opposed to "strategy." The popular prints depicting McClellan on the Peninsula seemed a joke to the editor, with their representations of "the second Napoleon mounted on a fiery black charger at the head of his troops, within a few yards of the bayonets of the enemy."[38] Indeed, political prints took up the partisan theme. A Currier & Ives political cartoon circulated after September 1862, called "Breaking That Backbone," contrasted the coming means of winning the war, "conscription" and "emancipation," with the methods that had so far failed to break the backbone of the monster rebellion. The failed means were exemplified in mallets wielded by McClellan and general-in-chief Henry W. Halleck and labeled, respectively, "Strategy" and "Skill."[39]

The groundwork for destroying McClellan's military reputation was laid in pamphlet literature that would endure—literally, as hard copy to be recirculated—into 1864, but the elections in 1862 did not themselves turn on the issue of McClellan's generalship. The career of Michigan Republican senator Zachariah Chandler serves to reveal what happened.

Soon after the failure of the Peninsular Campaign, Chandler began devising a well-documented destruction of McClellan's reputation. The senator had access to the confidential testimony before the Joint Committee on the Conduct of the War, of which he was a member and which had recently voted to allow public use of its testimony.[40] On

July 16, 1862, Chandler attacked McClellan in a long speech in the Senate. By the time of the dinner recess at five, Chandler had completed only his description of the Ball's Bluff disaster of 1861—"wholesale murder," he concluded. At seven, he resumed by tackling the Peninsular Campaign. He laid heavy blame on "spades and pick axes," which, employed "in malarious swamps," exhausted the army and exposed the men to disease. "We have lost more men by the spade than by the bullet," he charged. The argument proved particularly useful to antislavery men at the time, for they could point out the relief that could be brought to the army by employing the enemy's confiscated slaves to dig in the swamps. Unlike the Union army, the slaves were acclimated to these conditions (according to the crude public health assumptions of the era). Chandler maintained that such a policy would have saved 30,000 men. He derided "strategy" with bitter sarcasm.

The speech had the earmarks of an electioneering document. It had obvious local uses for Chandler, for he twice noted the contributions of Michigan regiments to the fighting and their being ignored in official dispatches. And his peroration condemned the "fools and traitors" who, Chandler predicted, were certain to criticize him for making the speech. "The traitors have been denouncing every man who did not sing paeans to 'strategy,'" he complained, "when it led to defeat every time. The traitors North are worse than the traitors South," for they were "stabbing their country in the dark."[41] Here was a typical transformation made by the two-party system: the opposition political party became an enemy more to be dreaded than the rebels in arms in Virginia.

Chandler's speech, though long, came near the end of the congressional session, when Republicans were rushing to pass important legislation. He admitted that the subject of the speech was "not . . . quite germane" to the bill being considered at the time, one for freeing political prisoners from military confinement. But Republicans made time for the speech, for they needed to get it on the congressional record before the recess to go home and campaign in the autumn elections. Then it could be printed at the Government Printing Office and circulated at federal expense, through the franking privilege, for partisan electioneering purposes.[42]

Chandler put the speech to use right away when he went home to Michigan, and he boasted of its success.[43] But problems soon intervened to hamper its usefulness. For one thing, after General John Pope failed at the Second Battle of Bull Run at the end of August, President Lincoln was forced to turn to McClellan again to command the Army of the Potomac and repel Lee's invasion of the North. That meant that Chandler's speech was now critical of the republic's defender, hand picked by the Republican president. Other issues crowded the political canvass as well, especially after the appearance on September 22 of the preliminary Emancipation Proclamation. But Chandler had laid the groundwork for two years hence; and as it turned out, the Republicans eventually destroyed McClellan's reputation in 1864 in exactly the ways Chandler laid out in the summer of 1862.

IT IS NEVER SIMPLE to separate the politicians' sincere sentiments from their hustings appeals. The revolt against "strategy" among Republicans, for example, added fuel to the simmering criticism of West Point and professional military men.[44] Yet, the anti-"scientific" part of the assault did not carry over into tangible opposition to the

United States Military Academy. West Point was, after all, subject to congressional budget votes, and Republicans held the majority in Congress; but they did not seriously attack the academy. When the funding bill came up in the Senate in the early days of 1863, for example, there was a long debate, but the bill was a foregone conclusion—it would pass by a landslide. No sane party wanted to destroy the nation's most important military academy in the midst of the greatest war in the nation's history.

Some Republicans could not resist denouncing the academy anyhow. Leading the rhetorical attack was Benjamin F. Wade of Ohio, who went so far as to say that "if there had been no West Point Academy, there would have been no rebellion. That was the hotbed in which rebellion was hatched."[45] Yet no Republican proved willing to argue here that war was not a science. Lyman Trumbull, professing that he was not "the advocate of ignorance, as against science," nevertheless voted against the bill and weighed in heavily on the side of the bayonet:

> To what do you owe the loss of thousands and tens of thousands of men who have sickened and died in the swamps upon the borders of rebeldom while they were engaged in constructing fortifications, except to the passion which these engineers had for constructing fortifications?
>
> Sir, what we want is generals to command our armies who will rely upon the strength of our armies . . . Let them, with their eyes fixed upon the rebels, advance upon them with the power of a hundred thousand bayonets, and you will put the

enemy to flight and to rout, and crush and destroy this rebellion. You can never destroy it by
building fortifications and planting cannon in
them and seeing how far you can throw a ball,
and if you can kill some man farther than you
can see him.[46]

Most speakers preferred to skirt the issue and dwell on the
academy's old Achilles heel—its "aristocratic" admissions
process and undemocratic nature. The bill passed the Senate
29 to 10.

Though never a critic of West Point and always a firm believer that the war had to be "conducted on military knowledge" rather than "on political affinity,"[47] President Lincoln
was perhaps more vexed and frustrated by McClellan's behavior than anyone else. Lincoln obviously shared some of
the Republican critique of the failure on the Virginia Peninsula, but as commander-in-chief, he knew things about the
Army of the Potomac that were not common knowledge,
and he focused his attention in the fall of 1862 on the problem of absenteeism.

At about the time of his October visit to McClellan's army
after the Battle of Antietam, Lincoln apparently became
alarmed with the great disparity between the actual number
of troops present for duty as compared with the numbers
listed on the army's rolls. Lincoln spent the rest of the autumn and early winter obsessed with that disparity—which
he blamed on the commander, McClellan. There are four impressive pieces of evidence bearing on the subject. First and
most important are the reports listing soldiers present
for duty that Lincoln solicited directly from officers in the
Army of the Potomac (thus bypassing their commander,

McClellan).[48] Next is a memorandum on the subject Lincoln drafted: "The Army is constantly depleted by company officers who give their men leave of absence in the very face of the enemy, and on the eve of an engagement, which is almost as bad as desertion. At this very moment there are between seventy and one hundred thousand men absent on furlough from the Army of the Potomac. The army, like the nation, has become demoralized by the idea that the war is to be ended, the nation united, and the peace restored, by *strategy*, and not by hard desperate fighting."[49]

The account of the president's behavior during a White House visit in November—our third piece of evidence—renders a sense of Lincoln's exasperation at the problem. Mary Livermore and other women associated with the United States Sanitary Commission called on the president looking for encouragement but instead got an earful of the same bitter complaint:

> I have no word of encouragement to give. The military situation is far from bright, and the country knows it as well as I do. The fact is, that people haven't yet made up their minds that we are at war with the South. They haven't buckled down to the determination to fight this war through; for they have got the idea into their heads that we are going to get out of this fix, somehow, by strategy. That's the word—*strategy!* General McClellan thinks he is going to whip the rebels by strategy, and the army has got the same notion. They have no idea that the war is to be carried on and put through by hard, tough fighting that will hurt somebody, and no head-

way is going to be made while this delusion lasts
. . . when you go back . . . you won't find a city on
the route, a town or a village, where soldiers and
officers on furlough are not plenty as blackberries
. . . General McClellan is responsible for the delusion that is untoning the whole army—that the
South is to be conquered by strategy.[50]

Finally, our fourth piece comes from the diary of Orville
Hickman Browning. In December he visited the president in
the White House at six in the evening and wrote afterward:
"Among other things, he said there was never an army in the
world, so far as he could learn, of which so small a percentage could be got into battle as ours—That 80 per cent was
what was usual, but that we could never get to exceed 60.
That when he visited the army after . . . Antietam he made a
count of the troops, and there were only 93,000 present
when the muster rolls showed there should be 180,000."[51]

It was fair enough for Lincoln to blame McClellan for the
problem, but it is curious that he attributed the absenteeism
to an infatuation with "strategy." Surely, in an atmosphere
not as saturated with increasingly partisan criticism of
McClellan for embracing "strategy," Lincoln might have
characterized the problem as one of discipline or morale.
But he did not; like other Republicans, he had absorbed the
party line on McClellan's failures. Lincoln did not distrust
Democratic generals, as many Republicans did, but he came
to distrust "strategy" all the same.

The culmination of the critique of McClellan naturally
came in the presidential campaign of 1864. Because of the
Republicans' careful early groundwork, they foiled the political strategy the Democrats had developed for the campaign.

McClellan was one in a long line of military hero candidates, generals who stood for nothing, nominated in order not to divide the party's followers over issues. Lincoln and the Whigs back in 1848 had used a similar gambit: nominating a popular war hero, Zachary Taylor, to capitalize on military glory gained in a war instigated by the Democrats. It worked for the Whigs, but in 1864 the scheme failed when McClellan's military reputation emerged in the canvass not as the Democrats' refuge and glory but as part of their political problem.[52] Republicans demolished the Democrats' major campaign offering, McClellan's official and long-awaited report of his campaigns. The architect of this demolition was a shrewd Republican newspaper reporter named William Swinton.

In April 1864 Swinton reviewed McClellan's report in twelve articles in the New York *Times* which served as the basis for his political pamphlet *McClellan's Military Career Reviewed and Exposed: Military Policy of the Administration Set Forth and Vindicated.*[53] Swinton cast a sharp eye over McClellan's report, looking for inconsistencies and for documents excluded but known to exist from the government investigations by the Joint Committee on the Conduct of the War. The reporter ridiculed the "tragi-comedy of the spade before Yorktown" and, echoing "Bull Run" Russell, noted that a "real charge with the bayonet" was "not to be looked for from any portion of [McClellan's] . . . army." Instead, "thousands of lives [were] lost by epidemics of the region into which our army had been led."[54]

Republicans at every level of public discourse attacked McClellan. On a higher plane than political pamphleteering, James Russell Lowell also reviewed McClellan's report—for the prestigious *North American Review*. Lowell rejected "with the contempt they deserve the imputations on McClellan's courage and his military honor." Nevertheless, Lowell said that McClellan had "every theoretic qualification, but no ardor, no leap, no inspiration. A defensive general in an earthen redoubt not an ensign to rally enthusiasm and inspire devotion."[55]

Benjamin F. Wade, in a rousing speech in New York City in October, made the infamous spade of Yorktown virtually treasonous: "The rebels knew how rapidly the Yankees could fall before the miasma of the swamps, and were glad to let them dig in quiet." Of Malvern Hill, Wade said, "Gen. McClellan simply rode along the lines of the army half an hour before the battle commenced, and then *withdrew with his staff on board a gunboat* . . . There he was, on a gunboat, amidst his wine and cigars, giving no attention to the operations in the field."[56]

The Republicans had many other arrows in their quiver with which to injure McClellan's military reputation.[57] All commentators faulted his exaggerations of enemy numbers, his insatiable appetite for reinforcements, and his constitutional slowness of movement. These accusations were on the mark and could hardly have harmed the war effort. The accusations about skulking at the rear while combat raged, about professional skill and strategy, about the reluctance to inspire bayonet assaults, and about the uselessness of fortification and entrenchment, on the other hand, were unfair and uninformed and could not have done the Union war effort any good. At worst, party needs here got in the way of the soldiers' needs for reasonable handling in battle and for protection from enemy shot and shell.

By late-summer, President Lincoln was as prone as any other Republican to dismiss the value of protective cover for

Union troops. When the Congregationalist clergyman Joseph Parrish Thompson visited Lincoln on September 6, the nation was awaiting McClellan's letter of acceptance of his party's nomination. The Democrats had strapped their war candidate to a peace platform, and McClellan was working in private through draft after draft of a letter accepting the nomination but wriggling free of the platform. The public did not yet know what he would say, and Thompson therefore lightly remarked to the president that McClellan seemed as slow in mounting his party's platform as he had been in taking Richmond. "I think he must be entrenching," the humorous president replied.[58]

The shovel was a Republican joke rather than a battlefield necessity even in this new era of high firepower. The Thompson anecdote had its uncanny illustration in the popular press, in a woodcut cartoon that appeared in *Harper's Weekly* on September 17, 1864. The cartoonist depicted Lincoln holding a diminutive figure of McClellan in the palm of his hand, and the punch line was "This Reminds Me of a Little Joke," a reference to McClellan's short stature. But what is also notable is McClellan's curious armament in the cartoon—a shovel.

The Republicans' criticism of McClellan particularly invited needless exposure of the officer class to enemy fire. McClellan was repeatedly depicted as "The Gunboat Candidate," the title of a Currier & Ives cartoon in which the general—astride one of the famous cavalry saddles of which he was the inventor, mounted on the bowsprit of a gunboat—watched battle on the far shore through a telescope. In another cartoon of the campaign, McClellan lolled back in a deck chair, sipping champagne, while his saber lay idle beside him. The subtitle of the cartoon told the viewer to "See evidence before the Committee on Conduct of the War."[59] The Union League of Philadelphia, a major source of Republican posters for the 1864 canvass, printed the *Deplorable Cowardice of M'Clellan, During the Battle of Malvern! The Gunboat Story again Confirmed!*[60]

UNDER THE PRESSURE of such virulent and steady criticism, the Democrats finally devised counter arguments. The most ingenious of these were developed by the editors of the New York *World* during the election summer— perhaps in consultation with the candidate himself, with whom the paper had close connections. Up to that time, the Democratic party had enjoyed the luxury of pointing out Republican failures in the war without having to explain precisely how Democrats would succeed if in control themselves. With McClellan now portrayed as the very cause of these early failures, something had to be put forward in answer.

The *World* began by defending McClellan's report. "The *Evening Post*," said the editors, "is fighting General McClellan's battles over again, and is endeavoring to revive an old prejudice against that officer because he did not attempt to carry the works of Yorktown by assault instead of by siege. The history of the war, however, since the siege of Yorktown, has completely justified General McClellan's military judgment on that occasion. There is not a conspicuous instance during the whole war of intrenchments being carried by assault, either by the Union or rebel armies."[61] Later in the month, the *World* drove the point home with the observation that "General Grant has blunted the edge of the ignorant derision of which the spade used to be made the butt. General Grant always entrenches; as do also the rebels."[62]

The *World*'s most analytical pieces were published in July:

> The fact which we pointed out a short time since, that intrenchments have rarely been carried by storm, by either the northern or southern armies since the war commenced, has attracted considerable attention . . . The difference in this, as compared with former wars, is caused by the use of rifled instead of smooth-bore muskets. *Armes de precision* first came into general use in the Italian war, and changed essentially the conditions under which battles were fought and sieges conducted. When the old "Brown Bess" was in vogue, armies could maneuver within sight of each other, out of range, and hence there was no necessity for the earthworks and intrenchments which are now indispensable when armies come into each other's vicinity . . . This very simple fact tells the whole story of the murderous but fruitless assaults which have been made by both northern and southern armies since the war commenced. There is not one conspicuous instance in all our sieges and battles where a successful assault has been made . . . Assaults upon fortified positions are hereafter to be set down as military crimes and blunders.[63]

By September the *World* had developed an elaborate defense of "strategy," the old Republican bugbear. The administration, the editors charged, had "deliberately repudiated foresight, circumspection, adjustment of parts and military science. It refused to put bravery under the direction of brains . . . For soldierly coolness it substituted ungovernable impatience; its 'art of war made easy' consisted of nothing but heedless, unreflecting courage. The administration having made this issue with General McClellan, the question between strategy and anti-strategy was committed to the decision of events."[64]

The *World* ingeniously recalled a public letter written by Secretary of War Stanton after the fall of Fort Donelson in 1862 and quoted from it to effect. Stanton had written:

> Much has recently been said of military combinations and organizing victory. I hear such phrases with apprehension. They commenced in infidel France with the Italian campaigns and resulted in Waterloo . . . We owe our recent victories to the Spirit of the Lord . . . Patriotic spirit with resolute courage in officers and men is a military combination that never failed.
>
> We may rejoice at the recent victories, for they teach us that battles are to be won now and by us in the same and only manner that they were ever won by any people or in any age since the days of Joshua, by boldly pursuing and striking the foe.[65]

It was the sort of letter that would confirm the Democrats' view of Republicans as fanatics, and it is little wonder the Democrats remembered it two years later. At the very least Stanton's letter left the administration vulnerable to withering Democratic criticism, which the *World* finally delivered in 1864:

They undertook to exalt anti-strategy by a practical demonstration of its advantages. They were going to have Pope march in a straight line to Richmond and snatch the prize from McClellan's slower grasp . . . [Pope failed at Second Bull Run.]

But Stanton's pious anti-strategy did not give in to this demonstration. The chagrin of seeing McClellan victorious [at Antietam] whetted the zeal of the administration to put down the French atheism of his strategy. Stanton bethought him of "the days of Joshua;" again insisting that "boldly pursuing and striking the foe" was the whole of military science worth knowing.[66]

The *World*'s editors recognized that the "scoffing at West Point ideas then prevailing among Mr. Lincoln's supporters" was certain to vanish, and did. Such words were seldom heard with West Pointers Grant and Sherman leading the attack.

As always, the *World* carefully avoided any appearance of lack of patriotism and found that paying a compliment to Sherman put the Republican administration in the pillory. These Democrats pointed out that in the wake of the fall of Atlanta to Sherman's armies,

General Sherman's brilliant campaign has been equally a satire on the 'spirit-of-the-Lord' fashion of fighting which was the instrument for supplanting General McClellan. General Sherman's splendid advance and glorious success testify, from beginning to end, to the worth of strategy. He has gained no important advantage by 'mov-

ing upon the enemy's works;' he has won the
most solid success of the whole war by a series of
grand maneuvers . . . The ignorant contempt of
West Point has vanished, because it was seen that
West Point science [in the hands of rebel gener-
als] was a match for our resources.[67]

IT MAY SEEM STRANGE that the Democrats'
military analysis, which actually did anticipate the entrenchments of World War I and the maneuver of World War II,
could not survive the Civil War. In fact, it died with the failure of McClellan to win the election in 1864. The Democrats
had no further use for the arguments, devised as they were to
defend a particular candidate who would never gain nomination for national office again. The party's main position in
the fall campaign centered instead on the Emancipation
Proclamation as the prime example of Republican policies
that divided the North and unified the South in stubborn
opposition. The racial antipathies embodied in such Democratic doctrine proved more useful in the Reconstruction
years that followed, as the party became increasingly white
supremacist.

But for a moment it is worth recovering the Democratic
viewpoint on military strategy in the summer of 1864, for it
reveals the fallacy of thinking of the Civil War as "modern,"
of thinking of the press as modernizing in its effect, and of
thinking of the Republicans as modernizers. It is worth being reminded of Stanton's Joshua letter with its belittling attitude toward "organizing" war.[68] Ironically, the Republican
political victory in 1864 buried for a century the military lessons of the Civil War. Party competition briefly caused a for-

ward-looking vision to surface among the desperate Democrats, but just as quickly caused it to be forgotten. And in the end, two-party competition had driven the Republicans to a dysfunctional critique of Civil War military operations. The two-party system proved to be the very death of strategy.

4

"Odious to honourable men"

The Press and Its Freedom in the Civil War

FREEDOM OF THE PRESS survived the Civil War, as the two-party system survived it—more or less in spite of itself. Vigilante mobs, unthinking generals, and politicians threatened press freedom in the North here and there and from time to time, but their actions were often egged on and in the end usually excused and artfully explained by influential newspapermen. The government did not systematically and as a matter of policy threaten to stop the presses (except in border states), and the judiciary almost never did so. But the press itself was a constant threat. Its partisan nature made journalists themselves serious enemies of freedom of the press in wartime.

Journalists devised many of the arguments for suppressing the dissenting press during the war. The judiciary steered well clear of formulating repressive doctrines, and the administration left explanations of suppression of press freedom to a War Department solicitor.[1] In some instances journalists not only rationalized government actions but urged that action be taken. The Republican press led the way, because Republicans controlled the administration and Con gress throughout the Civil War. But the partisan dynamic of mid-nineteenth-century journalism constituted the cause, and not anything inherent in Republican ideas, which tended to be liberationist and opposed suppression of freedom to criticize slavery in slave states. In other words, Democratic journalists would likely have done the same as Republicans did during the war if the parties had changed places.

Threats to freedom of the press in wartime were in many instances an outgrowth of competition between the two major political parties. Conversely, freedom of the press in war was not protected by the operation of the two-party system. The Republican press rarely offered any impediment to government attempts to silence newspapers. A few far-seeing journalists like Republican Horace Greeley eventually sensed the danger to press freedom posed by government in war, but far-seeing journalists were the exception under the conditions of a party press. And Greeley glimpsed the true interests of the fourth estate only briefly in 1863. Thus the two-party system, when linked directly to the press, as it still was in the middle of the nineteenth century, failed to ensure one of the essential guarantees of the United States Constitution and ultimately one of the conditions fundamental to the ultimate survival of the party system itself.

The hostility of the two-party system to press freedom in time of war is suggested by the contrast between the Union and the Confederacy. Though lacking a two-party system, the South saw its press sail through the war largely uninhibited by government.[2] And that accomplishment came in a culture long accustomed to disallowing any discussion of the slavery question and thus more prone than northern culture to countenance suppression of traditional American freedoms.

THE EXTREME PARTISAN nature of the American press gave it a notorious reputation abroad. To be sure, foreign observers often mistook democracy itself—with its high literacy rate and a consequent impulse in newspapers to pander to readers—rather than partisanship as the root problem of the American press. But they agreed that the result was bad. William Howard Russell, for example, was so demonized for his unfavorable coverage of the Union retreat from the Battle of Bull Run that he commented, "My unpopularity is certainly spreading upwards and downwards at the same time, and all because I could not turn the battle of Bull's Run into a Federal victory, because I would not pander to the vanity of the people, and . . . because I will not bow my knee to the degraded creatures who have made the very name of a free press odious to honourable men."[3]

Russell had no way of knowing the adverse effects of the Bull Run defeat on press freedom in the North, but in its wake authorities thought immediately of securing the border slave states by force, especially Maryland and Missouri. President Lincoln drafted a memorandum two days after the battle suggesting strategic action on several fronts and insisting, "Let Baltimore be held, as now, with a gentle, but firm, and certain hand."[4] By 1864 there was not a single Democratic newspaper in Baltimore.[5] As for Missouri, Senator Lyman Trumbull made sure the president saw a letter from Colonel John M. Palmer, who was stationed in Missouri with the 14th Illinois regiment. The excitable and garrulous Palmer, noting that the Bull Run defeat "demonstrates that we have a war on our hands, that is . . . to be settled by . . . leaden balls and cold steel," urged tossing the presses of the

St. Louis *Missouri Republican* and other treasonous newspapers into the river (despite its name, the *Republican* was an
opposition paper). Lincoln forwarded Palmer's letter to General John C. Fremont, who was in command of Union forces
in Missouri, for "special attention."[6] Within a month,
Fremont would declare martial law in the state.

Shutting down opposition newspapers in the border states
provoked little criticism from Republican editors. Instead,
publishers and intellectuals in the North moved in the late
summer of 1861 toward endorsing suppression of the press
under certain conditions. Not only did they endorse it after
the fact but they also supplied arguments in lieu of government explanation. The government and, more often perhaps, the generals and provost marshals acted; the press explained. It did not complain.

The three Republican newspapers in New York in 1861—the
Evening Post, the *Times,* and the *Tribune*—provide typical illus-
trations of the point. On August 26 the New York *Evening
Post,* for example, began to report the suppression of "seces-
sionist" newspapers and to argue that newspaper protests
against actions curtailing personal liberty only shielded "the
great northern conspiracy."[7] "How long shall it be," the editors asked, "before all are made to heed the simple truth that
*the constitution protects only those who acknowledge and support
it?*"[8] In the *Evening Post*'s pages appeared an expert apologist
to supply the necessary historical precedents. Benson J.
Lossing, of Poughkeepsie, a prolific author of popular illustrated histories of the Revolution and the War of 1812, compared "The Tories of 1776 and 1861. The Press during the Revolution. How the Liberty of the Press was Regarded in 1776."

Lossing noted the changing nature of journalism before
the Revolution from "mere newspapers" to popular vehicles

of political opinion. As "the quarrel between the mother country and the colonists advanced and waxed hot[,] party lines were more distinctly drawn. The newspapers took partisan positions," he noted. When the colonies revolted, the Continental Congress, George Washington as military commander, and state governments all arrested people regarded as disloyal and suppressed Tory newspapers. "Upon precisely the same principles of action, it seems to me," the historian concluded, "our government is justified in using vigorous measures against the abettors of this unprovoked and monstrous rebellion—the tories of our day." Lossing did not mention the Constitution and Bill of Rights, which were adopted subsequent to the Revolution, and that omission made it easier to reach his strident conclusion: he would regard *"every man who is not a hearty supporter of the government at this crisis, as a dangerous enemy to his country.* And I hold it to be sound morality and sound patriotism to make every traitor under that definition, whether in the form of man, woman, newspaper or pamphlet, feel the restraining power of the government."[9]

Henry J. Raymond's New York *Times* argued a constitutional position rather than a historical one: "The extremest statement of the liberty of the Press under the Constitution, in times of peace, does not imply the liberty of furnishing aid, information and incitement to the armed enemies of the nation in time of war."[10] In the midst of their campaign to justify suppression of disloyal newspapers, the *Times* still glibly celebrated freedom of the press. The newspaper took note of the guilty acknowledgment by its factional rival in the city, the *Tribune,* that their "on to Richmond" headlines had sent Union forces prematurely into battle at Bull Run. The *Tribune* thought the press should leave military matters to the generals and cease criticism. The *Times* responded with an article entitled "The Functions of the Press," noting that the "very object of a newspaper is criticism." "The printing press," the editors intoned, "has created modern civilization by challenging abuses hoary with age—by exposing errors which so long held mankind in bondage."[11] The arguments for a free press were ready to hand, but they were selectively applied.

For its part, the *Tribune* quoted the U.S. Constitution but quickly moved to the New York State Constitution, whose bill of rights ensured press freedom but also contained a statement about a newspaper's responsibility for what it printed—leaving the press in the state free from prior restraint but otherwise vulnerable to government suits for seditious libel.[12] "The right is clearly recognized and solemnly guaranteed," the *Tribune* concluded, "but all who would exercise it are authoritatively notified that abuses of it will subject the offenders to punishment."[13] In keeping with that position, the *Tribune* in September applauded the action of a Westchester County grand jury, which handed the circuit court an opinion that three county newspapers and two German-language newspapers in the city were "disseminators of doctrines which, in the existing state of things, tend to give aid and comfort to the enemies of the Government." The grand jury called for prosecution of the editors and proprietors if the papers did not desist.[14]

The action of the grand jury in New York led the postmaster general to ban the five newspapers from the mails.[15] One of them, the New York *News,* an organ of the conservative Democrats Fernando and Benjamin Wood, defied the administration by distributing the paper by private express services and by hiring newsboys—one of whom was arrested in

Connecticut. Even the independent New York *Herald* applauded the failure of the New York *News* to beat the administration's repression, and the Republican *Times* naturally expressed its lack of sympathy for the *News*.

This early episode in the war has, in our own time, caught the attention of the Chief Justice of the United States Supreme Court. As a modern American sensitive to questions of civil liberty, Justice William Rehnquist, who reported the case in his book *All the Laws but One*, was surprised by that lack of fourth-estate solidarity. "Remarkably," Rehnquist commented, "other New York newspapers did not rally round the sheets that were being suppressed."[16] It requires an institutional understanding of the nature of newspapers in the nineteenth century to interpret this case and the behavior of the press generally during the war.

In fact, despite various qualifications and conditions, not a single Republican newspaper among those I have examined from the Civil War period consistently defended freedom of the press; all at some time or other endorsed suppression of the press by the government. Obviously, many papers would follow the lead of the more prestigious Republican journals like the *Tribune*. Other newspapers tended to agree with the *Tribune* in desiring suppression of the licentious press by some sort of legal action (including military arrest under martial law), but in condemning mob action to shut down such newspapers. Journalists, when they sought constitutional grounds for their position, preferred to quote the definition of treason as giving aid and comfort to the enemies of the United States, as though that phrase qualified the guarantees in the Bill of Rights or state bills of rights. But they rarely noted the part of the Constitution's definition which insisted that treason consist of an "overt act."

By November 1861 the *Tribune* had devised a principle on which to justify suppression of the press. Defending the United States from criticism in the British press that the country was witnessing the beginnings of a remorseless decline and eventual fall of American liberty, the *Tribune* replied:

> It may happen, indeed, as a mere matter of military police, that the Government may feel compelled, during the existence of an actual war, to control the circulation of journals openly in the interest of the enemy; but the right to do this by no means implies the right to prevent an honest discussion of any public policy. No Government can be expected to become the common carrier, in a time of extreme danger, of libels aimed at its very life. But there is a wide distinction easily perceptible, between an attack upon a Government's existence and a criticism of its measures.[17]

The *Tribune* solution was a distinction based on content: the government could suppress those who justified rebellion but not those who, like the *Tribune,* criticized the mode of putting the rebellion down. It retained, basically, the old-fashioned idea that the government could punish seditious libel.[18]

This was a neater distinction than the administration made. In fact, the president made few distinctions in public policy statements. The War Department's legal expert, William Whiting, did not have much to say on the subject in his influential *War Powers of the President,* first published as a pamphlet in 1862 and expanded thereafter. Whiting was most interested in treason, confiscation, and emancipation, but he did assert, as one of the headings of his little book expressed it succinctly in the 1863 edition, "Civil Rights of Loyal Citizens in Loyal Districts Are Modified by the Existence of War." "If freedom of the press cannot be interfered with," Whiting said specifically, "all our military plans may be betrayed to the enemy." If we look at the state of opinion on the subject after the war was over, we still find a bias toward freedom of the press but a certain vague reservation as well. John Lalor's *Cyclopaedia of Political Science,* a repository of learned opinion published two decades after the war, stated that "political press prosecutions, instituted by the government authorities, have . . . ceased altogether in the United States. That the federal government retains a latent control over the press is, however, the conclusion to be drawn from the action of that government during the late civil war."[19]

Lincoln was not eager to suppress newspapers—at least, not after Maryland, Kentucky, and Missouri were secured for the Union—but he did not control all the authorities throughout the vast country who might exert, temporarily and locally, their power to end circulation of a newspaper. Congress did not supply a rationale, either. Specifically forbidden by the Bill of Rights from making laws interfering with freedom of the press, congressmen more than the executive (as commander-in-chief in war) or the states (which were unrestricted by the federal Bill of Rights but had constitutions of their own, of course) must have felt themselves excluded from entertaining any notions of press restriction and did not raise the matter prominently in the halls of Congress.

The judiciary steered well clear of the issue. After the Westchester grand jury action, Samuel Nelson, a U.S. Su-

preme Court justice on circuit, asserted flatly that "words . . .
do not constitute an overt act."[20] Nelson was a Democrat,
but judges, be they Democrats or Republicans, did not appear eager to encourage prosecutions for seditious libel or to
pronounce doctrines from the bench that would inhibit
press expression.

The press itself supplied the necessary doctrines. Thus the
Chicago *Tribune* on August 27, 1861, published an article by
Edward Everett in which he argued that "it is an absurdity in
terms, under the venerable name of liberty of the press, to
permit the systematic and licentious abuse of a Government
which is tasked to the utmost in defending the country from
general disintegration and political chaos."[21] With the publication of Everett's article, the *Tribune* joined the ranks of Republican newspapers opposed to freedom of the press in
wartime: "The seditious sheets must be stopped while the
war lasts."[22]

CONDITIONS FOR THE PRESS in the North
did not improve as the war progressed. And in general the
Republican newspapers followed a course of applauding or
excusing suppression of newspapers after it occurred. The
reaction of the Republican Chicago *Tribune* to the plight of
the Chicago *Times* in the late spring of 1863 is characteristic.
On June 1, 1863, General Ambrose Burnside ordered the *Times*
suppressed for repeated expressions of "disloyal and incendiary sentiments." After receiving advice from Illinois Senator
Lyman Trumbull and Chicago Congressman Isaac N. Arnold, both Republicans, President Lincoln decided to revoke
the order on June 4.[23] The *Tribune* chose to take a hard line
on the case, however. It criticized the president and his advis-

ers for revoking the military order and then chose to develop a systematic intellectual defense of suppression of newspapers in wartime.

Unlike the *Tribune* in New York, the Chicago paper did not focus as much on message as on medium. The editors began with an assertion of the "rightfulness and necessity of martial law in time of war" in cases where civil law was unequal to the emergency. They argued that had the *Times* been published in Louisville, Kentucky, and suppressed by Burnside, as it surely would have been, there would have been little complaint. And there should be no complaint about suppression in more northerly Chicago, they insisted, because newspapers were different from "words orally delivered either in private conversation or in public debates." If Copperhead politicians in Chicago ranted before an audience at the local Democratic club, it would do no harm. "No soldier would hear what they have to say; as not one of their listeners ever entertained the notion of jeopardizing his precious hide in his country's defense, no one would have been deterred from enlisting." They explained: "Orators at a safe distance from the scene of the strife, may, as a matter of policy, be suffered to rant and roar to their heart's content," but "disloyal printed matter, which speaks just as forcibly to the passions, the prejudices, the former partizan hates, and the fears of the soldier in New Mexico, Arkansas, or Mississippi . . . is always dangerous." The point, the editors said with almost legal precision, was that the potential for injury to the war effort and not the place of publication was the proper basis of the decision to suppress a newspaper.[24]

In time of peace, the *Tribune* supported freedom of the press—indeed, urged it as a necessity. Thus later, when the newspaper's editors looked forward to a reconstructed

South after the war, they insisted on freedom of speech and of the press as essentials of a viable democratic society compatible with the North. Considering what amendments to the Constitution might be needed at war's end, the editors argued that the federal government should guarantee by constitutional amendment freedom of the press "from being prohibited by the States," as it was guaranteed only against the interference of Congress at the time. "The slave States," the *Tribune* pointed out, "or the oligarchy, have since 1830 wholly suppressed first all advocacy of emancipation, then all advocacy of freedom in the territories, and finally all advocacy of the Union itself."[25]

Freedom of speech reached a crisis in the North in 1863. General Burnside's disastrous policies on civil liberty, which not only brought about the Chicago *Times* fiasco but also the notorious arrest of Democratic politician Clement L. Vallandigham for what he said in a speech in Ohio, looked ominous enough that Horace Greeley decided something had to be done to organize the press against government threat. He called a meeting of New York editors for June 8, 1863, and there devised a doctrine of press freedom in war.

> While we . . . emphatically disclaim and deny any right as inhering in journalists or others, to incite, advocate, abet, or uphold or justify treason or rebellion, we respectfully but firmly assert and maintain the right of the Press to criticize freely and fearlessly the acts of those charged with the administration of the Government, also those of all their civil and military subordinates, whether with intent directly to secure greater energy efficiency, and fidelity in the public service, or in

> order to achieve the same ends more remotely,
> through the substitution of other persons for
> those now in power.

The New York *Tribune* now specifically added a dimension of freedom of expression for the sake of political opposition and abandoned emphasis on the seditious content of controversial editorials. It sought refuge in geography instead, insisting that "any limitations of this right created by the necessities of war should be confined to localities wherein hostilities actually exist or are imminently threatened, and we deny the right of any military officer to suppress the issues or forbid the general circulation of journals printed hundreds of miles from the seat of the war."[26]

The New York resolutions represented the work of a bipartisan meeting which included not only such Republicans as Greeley and an editor of the *Evening Post* but also agents from such Democratic papers as the Albany *Argus,* the notorious peace-Democratic New York *Express,* and the *Journal of Commerce.* But the real story lay not in the measure of bipartisanship achieved in Greeley's meeting but in the measure still unattained: the New York *Times, World,* and *Herald* did not send representatives, and no permanent organization or even future meeting was arranged.

Moreover, the *Evening Post,* which was represented at the meeting, dissented from the final statement. "We should like to have seen in these resolutions a more decided recognition of the right which the constitution unquestionably confers upon the government to protect itself and the nation in times of 'invasion and insurrection,' even to the disregard of the courts and the infringement of personal liberties."[27] June 1863 thus demarcated the high-water mark of assertions of press freedom in the North during the Civil War. If editors of the Democratic *World* and the powerful *Herald* had joined the *Tribune* in endorsing resolutions on press freedom in war, then modern American journalism, if not the modern legal doctrines of freedom of expression, might have been born in the Civil War. But that did not happen, and American journalism receded into a familiar pre-professional and pre-modern partisanship.

The *Tribune* itself lapsed into the patterns of two-party journalistic hostility in the summer of 1864, after the Lincoln administration had briefly seized the offices of two other New York newspapers, the *Journal of Commerce* and the *World*, both of which were Democratic. The *Tribune* later laid claim to intercession with the administration to restore the newspapers to their owners and operators, but the dispute between the maligned newspapers and the government led later in the summer to a suit in court against the army officer, General John A. Dix, who had seized the papers, and the *Tribune* at that time published a long "Argument of an Amicus Curiae" in General Dix's behalf. The anonymous article justified the suspension of the opposition newspapers "by the Commander-in-Chief of the Army in a military district, in time of actual war." The article pointed out that only a year before, New York City had seen all authority overthrown by a mob from which the rebels had hoped for aid and comfort. "Inter arma silent leges is the true maxim," concluded the friend of the court, and asserted that the *World* "should be suppressed altogether."[28]

In January 1865 the *Tribune*'s editors no longer hid behind the anonymity of a guest column in their paper and affirmed in their own editorial space that the Catholic newspaper in

New York, the *Metropolitan Record*, should be suppressed. The *Record*'s editor had attended Greeley's meeting on freedom of the press back in 1863, but that only made worse his "ignorance" of the line that must be drawn between liberty of the press and advocacy of sedition. Every issue of the *Record* for two years, the *Tribune* maintained, contained editorials that were "openly, glaringly traitorous" and thus constituted full justification for "peremptory suppression."[29]

The independent press of the day took its cue from the partisan press. It covered politics almost exclusively during the war, though with less partisan animus, and failed to strike out on genuinely independent paths. The Philadelphia *Public Ledger*, for example, wasted little sympathy on the Newark, New Jersey, *Journal*, when General John A. Dix had the editor indicted for using incendiary language about conscription. The Philadelphians thought the punishment had "fallen in the proper place," that is, on the person who used the incendiary language and not on the paper's innocent readers influenced by the message.[30] The Philadelphia paper's position came close to the point made by the president in his popular appeal for support after the arrest of Vallandigham the previous year. "Must I shoot a simple-minded soldier boy who deserts," Lincoln asked, "while I must not touch a hair of a wiley agitator who induces him to desert?"[31] Later in the summer of 1864 when the New York *Daily News* stated that "the call of Mr. Lincoln for soldiers is not binding in law upon the people of New York," the *Public Ledger* concluded that this was aimed at creating "revolt," but added, philosophically, "The freedom of the press is certainly well illustrated in such newspapers, if its wisdom, discretion and truth are not."[32] The difference in reaction points to the importance of initiative in these matters. When General Dix took action, the newspaper excused it. When he did not, the paper resigned itself to tolerance.

The independent New York *Herald*, which had a worse record on freedom of the press than its Philadelphia counterpart, simply did not believe in freedom of the press in wartime and maintained a general tone of spitefulness that increased its zeal for the silencing of other newspapers. Thus the *Herald* applauded "military justice" when officers in the Army of the Potomac arrested correspondents of the rival papers the *Tribune* and the *Times* "for the untruthfulness or inaccuracy of their letters." The issue for the *Herald* lay not in any direct threat to military security, either. The *Herald* asserted only that the "reckless assertions" and "crazy theory" that so often marked the reports from those correspondents would "prejudice" the army's "gallant commanders" in the "eyes of the people."[33] The *Herald* also echoed the *Public Ledger* in denouncing "incendiary journalism," when the party press seemed to invite resistance to law. Newspapermen in New York City tended to be especially sensitive after the draft riots in their city in the summer of 1863.[34] And the spiteful *Herald* agreed in praising the indictment of the New Jersey newspaper editors and urged that such should be the fate of the editors of New York's *Tribune* and *Evening Post*.[35]

THROUGHOUT THE POLITICAL correspondence remaining from the Civil War one encounters letters written to politicians urging the suppression of newspapers said to print unpatriotic articles. In the excitement of the times, with doubts about the legitimacy of party opposition in war and with the uncertain and infant definition of freedom of the press, this is not surprising, perhaps. It is shocking, however, to find how often, after examination of the authorship of the letter urging suppression, the source turns out to be another newspaperman.

L. H. Funk of the *Miltonian* in rural Pennsylvania, for example, wrote the chairman of the Republican state central committee, Simon Cameron, after the presidential election of 1864 to thank him for a $100 check Cameron had sent in appreciation of the paper's services to the cause. No sooner had he acknowledged the money than Funk launched into a suggestion for future Republican policy:

> We all feel here, that the Administration should become more stringent on *home traitors,* that is rebel sympathizers in the North than it has been. You are aware that the sheet at Sunbury called the "Democrat" is notoriously bad in its principles, doing considerable harm to the good cause. Why, I often enquire, should not such sheets be suppressed, especially now, since we have evinced our power by an overwhelming triumph. We could suppress those sheets and not be charged with the idea that we suppress them on account of their influence, for it is proven we need not care nor fear what influence they may exert. Suppressing this sheet would not bring a cent additional into my pocket, but it pains me to see the editor fulminate his opposition . . . Every disloyal mouth and every treasonable sheet must be closed and suppressed, let it be called "tyranny" or suppression of "free speech!"[36]

The letter is striking for its author's willingness to flaunt the shibboleths of freedom and for his advocacy of desperate remedies when the situation was, by his own admission, no longer desperate.

Funk could lay claim to disinterestedness in the matter and felt it necessary to do so, but the union of self-interest with the illiberal opportunities offered by war was too much for some newspapermen to resist. We glimpsed in an earlier chapter a particularly malign example, when Samuel Young, editor of the Clarion *Banner,* wrote Cameron at the time of the 1863 senate contest in Pennsylvania to suggest that "William Alexander, Editor of the *Democrat,* member elect, is clearly guilty of discouraging enlistments, and we desire to know the moment when to have him safely removed to Fort Lafayette or some other safe place."[37]

Unthinking sentiments of revenge against rival newspapers were not always the work of small-minded and provincial editors who could hardly be expected to envision journalism as a separate estate of the commonwealth. Impulses to throttle opposition operated at the highest end of the spectrum of journalism as well. A case in point involves *The Independent,* the famous New York Congregationalist religious newspaper which laid claim to the largest circulation in the world for such a journal. In truth, it was not as independent as its masthead and religious mission might suggest. In the war *The Independent* supported Republican measures, and its editor, Henry C. Bowen, was a seeker of administration patronage. In the summer of 1862 Bowen asked for a letter of recommendation from Secretary of State William H. Seward in a quest to become the collector of revenue for Brooklyn. Bowen conceived of his religious journalism under the circumstances as political work, for a subsequent letter to the president is indistinguishable from many other requests for patronage for party work: "I have never asked a favor before, of the Government while I have been disposed to work in the front ranks, for more than a score of years, in the cause."[38]

And Bowen had the outlook of a partisan mid-century newspaperman in another important respect. After Lincoln issued the preliminary Emancipation Proclamation in September 1862, Bowen reacted to the New York *World*'s criticism of it by writing Seward excitedly and enclosing an editorial clipped from that Democratic newspaper with this comment, "In my judgment . . . a sheet that will give publicity to such sentiments as are contained in an editorial in to-day's World, should be *suppressed instanter.*"[39] Writing such a letter meant considerably more than venting spleen about the opposition at a café after work or even in the editorial pages of a paper. Bowen was writing on the letterhead of an influential newspaper to government officials who could give orders to suppress newspapers that would be obeyed by marshals or soldiers.[40]

As a journalist all his professional life, George Wilkes had, despite his political independence, absorbed the values of the era's culture of journalism. When he added political coverage to *Wilkes' Spirit of the Times* during the war, he accelerated his absorption in that culture, though he studiously refused to be connected directly with a party.[41] Early in 1863 Wilkes wrote to Salmon P. Chase advocating the restriction of circulation of the Democratic *World:*

> I have this morning written to Genl Hooker that
> large quantities of "The World" are daily sent in
> bulk for gratuitous distribution throughout the
> Army of the Potomac. I have likewise informed

him that these papers are filled with seditious appeals to the soldiers not to fight under the present programme of the Administration, and that unless we forbid their further introduction to his lines he may soon be without a camp.

Mr Stanton is very properly averse to any measures calculated to trammel the circulation of [papers?], but I think if you would speak to him now, he would see that this irregular, illicit and purposely mischievous distribution is not entitled to the consideration or immunities which apply to the ordinary laws of trade.[42]

Chase's response is unknown.

Lincoln's old political associate, Mark W. Delahay of Kansas, had a long career as a newspaperman before the war. But when he wrote the president to compliment him on his public letter to James C. Conkling, a key document for the 1863 Republican campaigns, Delahay excused himself for offering a note of criticism as well: "You are too easy and lenient with . . . Traitor Newspapers."[43] And R. W. Holloway, who was Indiana governor Oliver P. Morton's loyal private secretary during the Civil War, wrote Lincoln's private secretary, John G. Nicolay, a former newspaper editor from Illinois, in 1863 enclosing a paragraph clipped from the Democratic *Indiana State Sentinel* published in Indianapolis, as an example of the sort of thing regularly published in that paper. It "should be suppressed," he wrote. "We are upon the eve of civil war in Indiana, and you need not be surprised to hear of a collision here at any time."[44] Holloway became the editor of the *State Sentinel*'s Indianapolis rival, the *Indiana State Journal*, in 1864.[45]

The party's public leaders and candidates for high elective offices had rather different views from its henchmen who worked in the press or in the custom houses. When Hiram Barney read an article in the *Herald* in 1862 saying that McClellan should have more power in controlling the administration and the cabinet, he decided that it verged on being a call for caesarism and wrote the secretary of the treasury, "For this article the paper ought to be suppressed and its Editor imprisoned."[46] Not only did editor James Gordon Bennett of the *Herald* escape arrest and imprisonment, but the president took the view that he must be humored rather than suppressed.[47] Neither Lincoln nor Chase pursued Bennett's arrest.

Thus, the party leaders who were candidates for elective office held more advanced views on press freedom than the less visible partisans working at newspapers and in the custom houses. Chase's views had their limits in times of war. Asked by Henry W. Hoffman of Baltimore, the secretary treasurer of the Unconditional Union state central committee in Maryland, to help with the Republican platform for the state's elections in 1863, Chase advised him:

> The Platform should declare . . . in the most explicit terms, that there is no such thing in times of rebellion as supporting the National Government, without supporting the Administration of the National Government; that the administration of the National Government is confided, by the Constitution, to the President, assisted, in their several spheres of duty, by the Administrative Departments; and that, therefore, while the freedom of speech and of the press should not be

> arbitrarily infringed, the measures of the Presi-
> dent, and general policy of his Administration,
> should, under the present trying circumstances
> of the country, be sustained by all true patriots in
> a spirit of generous confidence, and not thwarted
> by captious criticism or factious opposition.[48]

Despite such views, here doubtless tailored to a border state, Chase hewed to the administration's basic view on freedom of the press and went even a little farther in his tolerant attitude. Chase opposed the arrest of Clement Vallandigham and the suppression of the Chicago *Times* and admitted only the standard administration exception to his position: "Except in some extraordinary cases such as existed in Maryland when too few arrests were made, the law in my judgment is sufficient and the regular processes of the law are sufficient."[49]

Chase generally expressed and acted on a sense of broad freedom of speech in cases arising above the border states. In 1864 Barney detained from shipboard three copies "of a work the subject matter of which is adverse to the administration, and in full sympathy with the rebels" imported by a bookseller named F. W. Christian. Chase noted that

> these copies were imported by Mr Christian with
> no desire to promulgate the doctrine of secession
> or to give publicity to disloyal sentiments; but on
> the contrary were designed for his loyal custom-
> ers whose position in the world of letters, made it
> necessary that they should know what was writ-
> ten abroad against the Government in order that
> they might the better refute all the calumnies
> when occasion required. Besides, I am not aware

of any law which prohibits the importation of books containing adverse criticisms on the Government.

The treasury secretary sternly ordered Barney to return the three books to Christian and admonished the custom house collector to "take care that zeal for the country does not degenerate into injustice towards individuals."[50]

ALTHOUGH REPUBLICAN newspapers often excused and sometimes fomented suppression of the opposition press, they do not seem to have had a strong sense of the volatility of the issue in a country with a Bill of Rights, popular slogans concerning freedom of the press, and a peacetime tradition of party newspapermen accustomed to speaking their mind with unrestrained vituperation. A sense of the dangers involved can be seen by examining the behavior of the Democrats at the time of the suppression of the New York *World* and *Journal of Commerce* in the bloody spring of 1864. Joseph Howard and Francis A. Mallison, reporters in New York City, concocted a scheme to enrich themselves by forging a presidential proclamation calling for a new draft of 400,000 men, which would cause public confidence in the North to fall—and gold prices to rise as a consequence. They would buy gold the day before and sell the day of the proclamation. They knew the tricks of the newspaper trade and managed to palm the proclamation off on sleepy Associated Press workers at four in the morning. Two Democratic newspapers in New York, the *World* and the *Journal of Commerce,* unwittingly published the bogus draft call.

The irresponsibly greedy plot triggered one of those moments when politicians revealed their worst suspicions about the opposing party. On May 18, 1864, President Lincoln ordered the seizure of the two newspapers' offices by soldiers. General John A. Dix, employing invalid corps soldiers, complied. The papers did not publish again until after the arrests of Howard and Mallison. The War Department allowed resumption of publication on the 21st. That the incident occurred in a state with a Democratic governor who was a contender for the presidency increased the dangers of confrontation.

In an editorial published in the newspaper shortly after the return of their offices, Manton Marble, the talented editor of the *World,* praised the Democratic governor's law-abiding restraint. Marble stated that when the newspapers were illegally suspended and their offices taken possession of by federal soldiers, Governor Horatio Seymour "had two courses open to him. One was, promptly to meet the trespassers on the threshold, by immediate restoration of the property seized by illegal violence; the other, to await the action of the tribunals, and proceed upon the solid ground of enforcing judicial mandates." The governor, he said, "wisely" chose the latter course "as the most consistent with the delicate relations which had arisen between two governments which have a common interest in maintaining with each other the most amicable understanding."[51]

The conflict between the Republicans and Democrats over this wrongful arrest was marked, but the incident also caused sharp conflict within the Democratic party in New York, not apparent in Marble's public editorials.[52] Because the editors and publishers were quickly exonerated when the true nature of the gold conspiracy was discovered, there was little time in May for the development of the full political conflict one might expect when the Republican President of the United States caused the suppression of the greatest Democratic newspaper in the land (the *World*) during a presidential election year. Instead, Governor Seymour sought a grand jury indictment in a New York court of the soldiers who had caused the arrests for kidnapping and inciting riot. The drama petered out in the summer with desultory thrust and parry by lawyers, General Dix, victims, and witnesses.[53]

Among the Democrats involved, the drama was much higher. Hard feelings developed between the aggrieved editor of the *World,* Marble, and Governor Seymour. When Marble failed to testify before the grand jury in the summer, the governor let him know that he regarded himself as having been left in the lurch. Marble answered the charge in a long and revealing letter.[54]

What Marble had written in his newspaper about the governor immediately after the crisis, as it turned out, had been a matter of maintaining solidarity in the party. In truth, the editor was wounded in his feelings because Seymour had not immediately telegraphed "his orders to the State Militia to eject the trespassers & restore to us our offices & protect us in the pursuit of our lawful business." It is a little chilling for us to see, once again, a moment during the Civil War when armed conflict might easily have broken out in the North over partisan differences. But Democrats off and on during the war flirted with the old idea that the militia was meant to be a counterbalance to the national army.[55] In general, they controlled so few state governments in that period that it did not much matter, but in New York in 1864 it might have mattered.

Samuel L. M. Barlow, who bankrolled the *World* and led the national Democratic organization in the presidential campaign of that same summer, apparently thought such a dangerous confrontation likely at the time of the suspension of the *World*. He played some role in attempting to bring it about. On May 20 he wrote the governor's henchmen, William Cassidy and Calvert Comstock, in consternation. He had thought on the 19th that the newspapers would be returned to their owners; but as nothing had happened then or the next day, he began "to fear that the adm[inistratio]n is willing to seize this opportunity to rid themselves of dangerous opponents." It would not surprise him, Barlow said, "if the interdict is made perpetual." He was not willing to rely on the courts because he was not sure that the courts could overawe General Dix and his soldiers. Barlow had heard rumors that martial law was to be imposed on New York City.

He warned the governor's office to "be fully prepared to preserve order as no evil that we can suffer is of much consequence in comparison with anarchy." The governor's measures "shd be prompt & absolutely decisive & some person entirely competent to preserve & restore order shd be placed in command in case there would be any necessity for adding the militia to the police force to suppress disorder."[56] Barlow, a part owner of the *World*, had become convinced, after three days of having his property illegally sequestered by the forces of the opposition, that the Republicans would not tolerate an effective opposition party and would opt for tyranny and anarchy instead.[57]

Manton Marble too retained some lingering fondness for the idea of state authority inserting itself to protect the rights of individuals against the great federal authority created by the United States Constitution. He told the governor's friends that, in his view, Seymour had missed his opportunity "to interpose the arm and shield of the State of New York between Mr Lincoln & the oppressed within the circumference of the State." Moreover—and now Marble's anger with the governor began increasingly to show itself—Seymour had been warned to "ensure the efficiency of the City Police for such a service when the occasion demanded." But nothing had been done. "You know," Marble wrote bitingly, "that men have been kidnapped from the streets of New York & other cities in the State almost daily ever since Gov. Seymour went into office. What hindrance has he ever interposed, what protest has he ever uttered. Have the Washington wretches learned to dread the power of the State of New York," he asked.

But Manton Marble was a different kind of man from S. L. M. Barlow. Marble was a true political operator, seeking in each situation partisan advantage, however devious. What the governor's "inaction during those two days" meant to Marble was that Seymour had lost "his best opportunity to strengthen the Democratic party, & put himself indisputably & singly at its head. He could not have contrived a better case for prompt decisive official action. He ought to have executed the laws, vindicated the sovereignty & asserted the jurisdiction of the state ostensibly by force of arms without the slightest danger of an armed collision; he might have had a direct conflict with the Washington authorities with an absolute certainty of victory—he could have heartened his friends and disheartened his enemies."

Doubtless what was deeply wounding in this letter was its hidden message: Marble was explaining why the *World* was working hand in glove with Barlow to make George B. McClellan the Democratic presidential nominee that summer—and not Governor Seymour. He was saying that the

World thought Seymour had flunked the test of party leadership.

That Marble would choose such a moment to identify presidential timber is immensely revealing. He saw in the suppression of the *World* and *Journal of Commerce,* as he likely saw in all public events, opportunity to create political image and exploit partisan advantage. That is what the press existed to do. It did not strike him that he was playing with fire. He dismissed out of hand the chance of genuine "armed collision" coming out of the confrontation between New York's militia and General Dix (yet only ten months had passed since the city's shocking draft riots). His position in the affair was analogous to Simon Cameron's in his attempt to win the Pennsylvania senatorship in 1863. Such partisans were willing to engage in brash and astonishing brinksmanship—without making any concessions to the times. One never has a sense with such men that perhaps the more daring and dangerous political methods might be left for peacetime and such risks should not be run when the republic was in genuine peril of destruction. Politics as usual might be dangerous, but many politicians exercised not one iota of caution.

The three Democratic politicians involved in the episode reveal the spectrum of partisan attitudes of the Civil War period. Barlow, after three days' trial, concluded that the conflict was likely real and not "just politics," to borrow Eric McKitrick's unfortunate phrase, and that the Republican administration was out to eliminate the loyal opposition. He sought an effective commander for the state militia to resist the federal forces of the Republicans. Barlow had returned politically to the era of the early republic, and he confused opposition with tyranny.

Marble automatically dismissed the likelihood of genuine violent conflict and sought to extract from dramatic confrontation with the government as much political advantage for Seymour's image as possible. He would engage in politics as usual even when the usual risked armed confrontation in order to shape the image of the opponent as a tyrant and of Seymour as a savior of liberty through states' rights.

At the other end of the spectrum stood Governor Seymour, who cautiously waited the development of events, opted for seeing what the courts would do, and sought in the end to reap what political advantage he could for the loyal opposition party before the grand jury months later in the election summer. Seymour had deep partisan differences with the Republicans but wanted to have irreconcilable differences referred to the courts. He habitually sought legalistic solutions, as he did for the questioned constitutionality of conscription in the state that had been home to the draft riots of 1863.

WHEN REPUBLICANS threatened the freedom of the press, as many did willingly and righteously, Democrats, even seasoned veterans of politics, men who were leaders of the national party, responded in ways that tested the boundaries of—and sometimes went beyond—what we now expect from the normal operation of the two-party system. Some sought finality in legal and constitutional settlements. Others risked violent confrontation between armed forces representing state and national authorities for the sake of political advantage. And some assumed that it was time to resist the opposition with armed force.

5

"Times of corruption and demoralization"

THE FUTILITY OF A LOYAL OPPOSITION

ONE OF THE LIABILITIES of our historical fixation on the accomplishments of the two-party system during the Civil War is that it blinds us to the framing role of the Constitution in the Civil War. With the possible exception of the depth of Confederate resolve, nothing shaped the Civil War more than the United States Constitution. For the war effort, the most important provisions were Article II, section 1, establishing the four-year term for the president, and Article II, section 2, making the president the commander-in-chief of the army and navy. In other words, the president would be commander-in-chief even if a war began with his inauguration and lasted four years—which, minus about six weeks, is exactly what happened after the election of 1860. I could find no one during this period who questioned the fact or wisdom of these provisions.

The four-year term for the commander-in-chief proved crucial to the Union war effort, for initial Union assaults on the Confederacy failed to bring decisive victories. The Constitution nevertheless dictated that a Republican determined to fight to keep the southern states in the Union would control the army and the navy for four years. The constitutional check on this executive power had proved of little practical use in American history after the Battle of New Orleans in 1815. Every major political party in the United States feared the fate of the Federalist party, which had disintegrated as a result of its opposition to the War of 1812 and the failure of its members in Congress to vote supplies. So during the Civil War, Congress's power to raise and support armies was not likely to be used in any way except to provide the president with the troops and supplies he needed to fight the war.

Goldwin Smith, a British observer sympathetic with the North, recognized this when he remarked of the presidential office (much too democratic an institution for his taste) that it had been set up in imitation of monarchy as "the republican counterpart of a king; which, though it has accidentally been of great service in this extremity, by giving the nation a sort of constitutional dictator, is, under ordinary circumstances, a dangerous stimulant to senseless faction and personal ambition."[1]

The Constitution thus substantially determined the nature of the political opposition during the Civil War—which was essentially useless. The Democratic party proved generally powerless and ineffectual in shaping the course of the war before the end of the president's term.[2] And since this war began at the beginning of a presidential term, it was widely assumed that the opposition party could have no effect on the war at all, since it would be over well before the next presidential election. A very long war, lasting as many as four years, could not be much affected by the opposition, even if it managed to elect additional members to Congress two years into the war. Under these constraints many Democrats naturally grew frustrated.

Because the Constitution gave the opposition party almost no role in war, the two-party system mattered less to the war effort than is often thought. That constitutional fact of life has been reflected unconsciously in the historical literature, which offers few studies of the Democratic party during the Civil War.[3] It has never been easy to play the role of the opposition party during an American war. The Federalists, largely confined to New England by the time of the War of 1812 and uncompetitive for the presidency, "experienced," says political historian Richard P. McCormick, "a keen sense of political frustration, amounting to a sense of loss of their political efficacy."[4] The Federalists' sense of frustration prefigured the hapless Democrats of the Civil War era in some ways, but McCormick underestimated the underlying constitutional cause of the opposition's plight: the war powers of the president. The Federalists vented their frustration in voting against supplies, threatening secession, and keeping militia forces confined to state borders—and paid the ultimate political price: disappearance from political competition after the war.

The course taken by the Democratic party during the Civil War testified to the culture's internalization of the Constitution over the years since the War of 1812. Like the Federalists, the Democrats not only faced the formidable war powers of a president they despised, but they were in a hopeless minority in Congress and, in most states, at the polls. Nevertheless, unlike the Federalists, the Democrats never devised a Hartford-convention array of proposed amendments to the Constitution to change the political system. The New England

Federalists had proposed amendments—obviously aimed at the Virginia dynasty of Jeffersonian Republicans—to limit a president to one term in office, to prohibit one president's succeeding another from the same state, and to base representation in Congress on only the free white population.[5] Democrats in the Civil War era took the political system as given in the Constitution and never dreamed of altering it. The Constitution stood formidably athwart their ability to affect the war effort.

Though that constitutional point may seem obvious, it has essentially eluded historians in their thinking about the role of political parties in the American Civil War. In fact, the great historian David Potter, who was the first to call attention to the role of the customary competition of the political parties in shaping northern success in the war, based his argument on a premise that defied this simple piece of constitutional logic. Speaking of the absence of a two-party system in the Confederacy and the consequent lack of importance of the off-year elections in the South midway into the war, Potter said:

> Alternative leadership at that point, or even earlier, might have found a very substantial backing and might have been able to dominate policy. But the absence of a two-party system meant the absence of any available alternative leadership, and the protest votes which were cast in the election became mere expressions of futile and frustrated dissatisfaction rather than implements of a decision to adopt new and different policies for the Confederacy. Thus, the political leadership could

> not be altered, and Jefferson Davis continued to
> the end in his distinctive role . . . the role of the
> leader of a Lost Cause.[6]

And Lincoln in his, it might be added, as the leader of a victorious cause—for the exact same reason. Leadership in the war effort could not be altered in either the North or the South by congressional elections, as the Confederate Constitution copied the U.S. Constitution's provisions on the president's power as commander-in-chief.

Potter's description of the futility of the elections was as true for the North with its two-party system as it was for the South without one. Despite increasing their vote in the North in the autumn elections of 1862, the Democrats could not "dominate policy" in the North. So President Abraham Lincoln did not renege on the Emancipation Proclamation, announced before those elections and put into effect after them. He did not end the policy of trials by military commission for persons in the North arrested for interfering with conscription—also the subject of a much-criticized proclamation on the eve of the 1862 elections. The northern opposition, though efficiently organized in the oldest political party in the world, was no less "frustrated" than the disorganized critics of Jefferson Davis.

Historians who have exaggerated the effectiveness of the two-party system during the Civil War have confused such a system with something entirely different, a parliamentary system instead of a constitutional one. The effects of a parliamentary system, North or South, would have been much as David Potter indicated: "alternative leadership" would have "been able to dominate policy" in dramatic fashion at least by 1862. Under a parliamentary system, if the Lincoln administration had not fallen in August 1861, after the shocking defeat at Bull Run and the humiliating flight from the field in Virginia to Washington, it would certainly have fallen late in 1862 after the traumatic failure of McClellan before Richmond in the summer.

In fact, the loss at Fredericksburg on December 13, 1862, did finally bring on a pale imitation of a parliamentary no-confidence vote, when Republican members of the U.S. Senate—the only members that mattered under the circumstances—attempted to force change on the administration between presidential elections. Even America's rigid constitutional system could not go unfazed by such a string of mortifying military setbacks, and the cabinet reached a major crisis, as Republican members of Congress attempted to drive William H. Seward from his office as secretary of state for allegedly paralyzing the military will of the administration. That internal party shake-up failed, and the success of the congressional insurgents, in any event, would not have brought Democratic influence to bear on the Lincoln administration but rather more radical Republican influence, under the leadership of Salmon P. Chase, who, from within the cabinet, egged on the movement to oust Seward. Short of resignation, impeachment, or assassination, Abraham Lincoln was going to fight the war, and he would have one faction or the other of the Republican party in Congress behind him, determined to fight the southerners.

The Democrats, though actually victims of the Constitution in many ways during the war, showed little interest in changing it. Significantly, their one approach toward a parliamentary system was a bill that would allow cabinet members to have seats in Congress. The bill was proposed by Democrat George Pendleton, of Ohio, in February 1864, with the avowed purpose of reducing executive power. In the debate that ensued, it became clear that congressmen could not decide whether giving cabinet members seats would strengthen or weaken the executive. Nothing came of the proposal.[7]

IF WE EXPECT the two-party system in the Civil War to have developed alternative leadership and refined new and different policies for guiding the war to a successful conclusion, as David Potter did, then we will be as disappointed in the North as he was in the South. Such a model is inadequate for opening up the world of the Civil War Democrats. And for that reason their world has remained substantially closed to us. The model makes us expect something rational, but the Democratic party in much of the Civil War North was irrationally disaffected from society.[8] Theirs was often a bewildered world of powerless frustration and their vision of society a bleak phantasmagoria induced by a political reality substantially unalterable for years.

Active political opposition during the war did not necessarily yield a practical ideology and leaders touting effective programs. Many Democrats suffered a fever dream of frustration and disbelief that America could have become so altered. The eloquence of the best-known parts of Abraham Lincoln's Second Inaugural Address has obscured his testimony to the sense of astonishing change brought about by the war: "Neither party expected for the war, the magnitude, or the duration, which it . . . attained. Neither anticipated that the *cause* of the conflict might cease with, or even before, the conflict itself should cease. Each looked for an easier triumph, and a result less fundamental and astounding."[9] Parties out of office rarely had to observe changes as dramatic and rapid as the ones the war brought, and the Democrats' reaction was more extreme than that of parties out of power in ordinary times. Eric McKitrick's description of the nature of the political opposition in the partyless Confederacy just as aptly describes this Democratic party opposition in much of the North: "It was not 'an' opposition in any truly organized sense. It was far more toxic, an undifferentiated bickering resistance, an unspecified something that seeped in from everywhere to soften the very will of the Confederacy."[10]

We can best glimpse the Democrats' "toxic" vision, born of political frustration, by reading the daily party press, and none offers a better view than the newspaper with the largest circulation in central Pennsylvania, the Harrisburg *Patriot and Union*. Marooned in the central part of the state between the metropolis of Philadelphia and growing Pittsburgh, Harrisburg was a provincial town that also contained the state capital. The life of the city was politics.

The *Patriot and Union* was dyspeptic and sour. By 1864, with a presidential election in the offing at last, Democrats could actually hope to alter national leadership and affect the conduct of the war, but years of discontent had taken their toll. Even patriotic poetry—the sort of doggerel that newspapers in the Civil War published from time to time—drove the editors to distraction. In February 1864 the *Patriot and Union* devoted three columns of vitriolic denunciation on its front page to Frank Moore's little patriotic gift book called *Lyrics of Loyalty*. To the Democrats of Harrisburg it was a "thoroughly Yankee book. The muse that inspired it . . . lurks about Plymouth Rock and feeds on codfish balls. The 'Lyrics'

. . . present every shade of Abolition folly and devilishness."
Poetry mentioning emancipation conjured up "the prospect
of elevating millions of enthralled blacks to luxury, laziness
and good clothes." The sarcasm was scathingly unrestrained.
An editorial on "War and Money" published in the same issue of the newspaper lamented the passing of the early
months of the war when a genuine willingness to sacrifice expressed itself throughout the American public. Now, snarled
the Democrats, they saw a "moral degeneracy" in the "fever
of prosperity which seems like a sudden dream to be passing
over the North."[11]

All areas of the North that were situated near assembly and
training camps for the vast Union armies, as Harrisburg was,
endured upsetting experiences with the raw youths who
came in from the countryside to prepare for war. Free at last
from parents, wives, and preachers, many of the young soldiers drank, gambled, visited prostitutes, and quarreled vio-
lently. None of the literate public was amused by this behavior, and from Detroit to Washington it drew dismayed
comments. For some, it invited sermons on temperance. For
Democrats, it symbolized the nightmare world created by
the Republicans.[12]

By March 1864 the Harrisburg *Patriot and Union* saw America as a "national Carnival," and terms like "debauchery" and
"Saturnalia" appeared in its editorials.[13] Indeed, debauchery
became a theme the editors attempted to illustrate from vi-
gnettes of social life in their own city and eventually
throughout the North. Their "Local News" section one day
offered "A Picture" of the demoralization existing in the city:
soldiers with money from enlistment bounties, and prostitutes—usually called "Cyprians" in the Harrisburg press—
ready to earn it from them. The editors adopted this vision

from the correspondent of a small-town newspaper, the Hollidaysburg *Standard,* and the state capital shared the small-town view.[14] The local news of the Harrisburg newspaper reported "Another Murder," "Another Soldiers' Riot," "Mob Law in Lebanon," and "Serious Affair in Washington, Pa.—Street Fight between Soldiers and Citizens."[15]

To catch the Democrats' attention in this dismal period the event need not have any overt political significance, as in the cases of soldiers attacking local Democratic offices. Instead, the section of the newspaper devoted to local news paid particular attention to assaults on citizens by soldiers in acts of ordinary crime.[16] It was as though the soldiers themselves became the representatives of the new society the Democrats hated under a Republican wartime administration. The tempting presence of soldiers awash in bounty money attracted thugs from Philadelphia who came to Harrisburg to prey on them.[17]

Finally, on March 11, the newspaper offered "A Pen Photograph of the Capital City" in what might be called mock-booster style:

> Here is a pen-picture of the Keystone capital, as it is, in these times of corruption and demoralization. The city is full of people; full of representatives and misrepresentatives; full of peachers [informers] and gamblers . . . full of men who pick individual pockets and get arrested, and men who pick the national pocket and get rich; full of private sharpers against whom the traveling and sojourning public is solemnly warned in placard, and the public sharpers who are deemed highly reputable because they do business on a large

scale; full of men who pay their pew rent regularly, thumb their hymn book religiously, and sell shoddy overcoats to soldiers; full of men who would not let a note go to protest for the world but have no scruples against mouldy bread and spoiled beef for any purposes; full of officers who could crush the rebellion instanter, were fierce mustaches and fancy uniforms of any avail against the rebels and rifles; full of officers who ought to [be] with their commands, and officers who never should have had a command to begin with; full of speculators and peculators; full, too, of ladies; ladies who are handsome and accomplished, and know it very well, and ladies who are homely and unaccomplished, and don't seem to know it; full, too, of females who are not ladies, though they now and then make an uninitiated member of the Legislature believe they are; full of cyprians of high and low degree, from the owners of gaudy equipages and the occupants of palatial residences, to the poor pedestrians who live in garrets; full of everybody and everything. An accurate pen-photograph of Harrisburg city, as it is to-day, would be a difficult achievement—as well attempt to paint a chaos, make a portrait of Proteus, or fix the figure of the fleeting air.[18]

It is difficult to reconcile the Democratic vision of social corruption relentlessly offered in these bitter reports, mostly locally inspired, with political scientists' models of two-party competition as we understand it today. Nor do the Harrisburg Democrats fit neatly into a scheme of historical analysis that emphasizes the eternal tug-of-war between those within the Democratic party who wished to maintain the purity of its platform message and those who wished to make politic adaptations of their appeal to the people.[19] The central Pennsylvania Democratic party and their banner newspaper, the Harrisburg *Patriot and Union,* in fact represented not the party's extremists but its moderates, for they were touting General McClellan as their presidential candidate and appealing for unity within the party from February of 1864 on. The extremist, pro-Southern, pro-peace, and sometimes pro-slavery wing of the party was anchored in the eastern part of the state, in Philadelphia.[20] The fevered vision belonged as much to the moderate war wing of the party as to the radical peace wing.[21]

The Harrisburg paper's disaffected stance continued throughout the election year, and it had parallels in the Democratic press elsewhere in the United States. The Detroit *Free Press,* for example, complained of the prevalence of crime in that city of the Old Northwest, and the Albany *Argus* in New York agreed that such social evil was "one of the legitimate and inevitable consequences of war." To Democrats, it seemed morally topsy turvy to go about freeing slaves when such rot had set in at home. "Never mind what becomes of the 'sanctity of the family circle,' let 'young men and boys'—young women and girls—go on 'sowing the seeds of moral and physical disease,' while Abolitionism holds high carnival over the land." New Yorkers like Pennsylvanians saw "the moral leprosy fastening itself upon the nation; the frightful increase of crime and prostitution; the penury, the woe, the suffering and death the war is causing."[22]

"Moral leprosy," echoed central Pennsylvania's Democrats, in their similar invocation of "the sad picture of moral desolation that is sweeping over the land. It is the moral and physical pestilence that follows closely on the heels of war."[23] This opposition world view had a dark explanation for almost everything. If the economy seemed prosperous, it was but a "bubble," said the *Ohio State Journal,* recalling to mind perhaps the South Sea Bubble that had so dismayed the English opposition in the eighteenth century and was echoed in America.[24] Pennsylvania Democrats saw in "the Stock Bubble" the "mania which seems to possess Americans as a people to acquire wealth rapidly," and it had "never been more fully exemplified than during the past three years."[25]

Miscegenation—a term coined by Democrats in 1864 and redolent of opposition frustration—remained the great symbol of moral inversion, but every institution was tainted in these Democratic eyes—schools, churches, and government alike. The public schools had a "leprous disease" and "moral plague."[26] Religion seemed completely abolitionized and could not be counted on to uphold private morality.[27] The nation's capital epitomized the nation's problems. "In the palmy days of southern rule, of slavery, there was not half the corruption there is now" in Washington.[28] Scandal among the new female employees of the Treasury Department became a Democratic fixation, a symbol of the nationwide problem of wartime prostitution. Harrisburg was full of carriages with officers riding flagrantly with "cyprians," and Washington, it was said, "literally reeks of prostitution, corruption and all manner of wickedness." The nation's capital had become "the Sodom of America."[29]

The sexual obsessions seem striking. Such a pattern of images matches the "themes of countersubversion" identified by the historian David B. Davis as a powerful ingredient in American political discourse in the antebellum period. The

Democratic editors of Harrisburg could be said to have "projected their own fears and desires into a fantasy of licentious orgies," to borrow Davis's description of the literature attacking Masons, Mormons, and Roman Catholics in the decades before the Civil War.[30]

In a remarkable development, Democrats in Harrisburg briefly reversed their customarily welcoming attitude toward immigrants to America's shores and began to worry about the decline of "native stock" in the country. The war's shocking casualties exhausted the population, and the Republicans were encouraging immigration to fill the gaps. The Democratic press in Harrisburg saw a "social revolution . . . certain to result from the intermingling of such a large and divers foreign element among our depleted native communities."[31] "The character of our people will be entirely changed," they warned, and "the 'new nation' thus created will not be exactly like that which is contemplated by the Abolitionists." The addition of four million African Americans to full citizenship would complicate the picture even more. Perfect equality among such citizenry seemed unlikely to the Democrats, and the only alternative, then, was the "clans and factions" of a Mexico-like nightmare.[32]

Against this background of sour disaffection, the *Patriot and Union* carried forward the regular activities of a presidential canvass—issuing calls for "available" candidates, pleas to keep the platform moderate, and constant exhortations to the faithful to organize. The nearer the date to go to the polls, the more the pages of the newspapers featured the familiar warnings to avoid deceptive practices of the opposition at the polls and to vote. Such routine features of American "political culture" persisted in 1864, but to fix our gaze upon them risks purchasing reassurance about the soundness of the two-party system at the expense of overlooking such critical developments in the campaign immediately at hand as the Democrats' apparently deep disaffection from Republican rule in central Pennsylvania in the middle of the Civil War.[33]

Leaving central Pennsylvania behind, we can say that even the most famous and most sober of the calls for Democratic party organization in 1864 bore a trace of detachment from political reality during the war. The *Address to the People of the United States, and Particularly to the People of the States Which Adhere to the Federal Government,* issued by Democratic members of Congress on July 2, 1864, raised many issues that could be used against the incumbent Republican administration—conscription, African-American troops, and government paper money, for example—and the pamphlet ended with a justification of and call for organizing an opposition (as if the Democrats were not already organized). However, the *Address* can hardly be regarded as an altogether serious exercise in alternative policy formulation. After all, it did not answer the most important question in 1864: what to do about the war. Over questions of war and peace the Democratic party was deeply divided and by no means willing to express an opinion until nearer election day, when the war's outcome might be more certain.

Moreover, the emphasis on "corruption of race" and the very last words of this generally sober statement of the political opposition betrayed the frustrated detestation of modern life that characterized much of the powerless opposition in the war. The Democratic members of Congress called for a restoration of Democratic control of the national government. "Then," they said in their concluding sentence, "will the laws be kept; then will free individual action be permitted and permissible; crime only will be punished, and harmony and peaceful relations and widely-diffused prosperity succeed to violence, intolerance, waste, bloodshed, and debauchment of the national life!"[34] That word "debauchment" had its roots in the obsessions with prostitution and corruption and moral inversion that characterized the world view of many on the opposition side during the war, from Harrisburg to Washington.

Not all Democrats expressed such deep disaffection as the Pennsylvanians did. A great variety of responses to Republican rule can be found in the party press. In Cleveland, for example, the *Plain Dealer* was enthusiastically, even uncritically, patriotic about the current generals in the field and the Union cause in current campaigns and about the locally recruited regiments. The newspaper was boosterish about the local community and seemed to regard the nation as essentially sound. These Ohio Democrats focused their criticism narrowly on Abraham Lincoln and pointed to broad social problems only in dealing with race. The *Plain Dealer*, too, supported McClellan for the party's presidential nomination. Likewise, the columns of the Democratic *World* seldom sounded the deeply disaffected note.

It should be remembered, however, that all the newspapers sampled here represented the pro-war McClellan wing of the party and eschewed the suicidal antics of the antiwar Democratic press. There readers could find the speeches of such party leaders as Benjamin Wood, Fernando's brother and a member of Congress from New York. "I have never voted a dollar for the war," Wood boasted in 1863. And he said that he foresaw at war's end "two great republics, expanding to grandeur, moving side by side upon principles almost identical, extending the area of self-government, the one northward and westward, the other southward and westward, united for mutual defense."[35]

Peace and war men alike worried first and foremost about getting elected, and so they carefully avoided making commitments on issues or candidates that might be rendered obsolete by the changing circumstances of the war. Thus the great symbolic head of the peace Democrats, Clement L. Vallandigham himself, thought the Democratic presidential nominating convention should be postponed to the late summer.[36] The true dynamic of party opposition during wartime was not formulating alternative policies but waiting and watching and committing to as little as possible. The *Patriot and Union* noted in the spring of 1864 that a July date for a national nominating convention came

> too early in the military history of the approaching season. The operation of our arms, their failure or success, must have a profound effect upon the popular bias in the Presidential election. No political party can win which does not regard such signs of the times as the history we are making so rapidly affords. No platform can succeed if not made somewhat in conformity to the temper of the present . . .
>
> The Democratic party by its action at Chicago may found its perpetuity or bring about its ruin . . . A declaration for peace, in the advance of a successful campaign or in the midst of it, would bring, for example, nothing but derisions about our ears . . . If we fail this time we may not live for the next four years . . . Let those at Chicago give us the *most available* man and a platform dictated

by the same principle . . . If it need be a successful
military chieftain to overthrow the chosen champion of Abolitionism . . . let us have him. If we
must cry war to elect him, let us cry it as lustily as
our opponents. In a word, the time has gone for
standing upon nice points.[37]

If events in war moved too quickly and unpredictably for
an opposition party to want to be pinned down on major issues, the risky obverse of the impulse to wait as long as possible lay in the disadvantages an opposition faced in a brief
electoral campaign. The Democrats in the Civil War, weak in
Congress and lacking control of many governorships or legislatures, needed a long campaign season to compensate for
the natural advantages of so many incumbent Republicans.

Despite such risks, the opposition enjoyed the luxury of
criticism without the burden of government responsibility.
Add frustration to evasive tendencies and the results in policy formation were often of little potential use to the republic. The organizational development of policy alternatives
followed the grassroots convention process from county to
state to national nominating conventions. The resolutions
drafted at the low-level delegate conventions, dutifully
printed in close type by the party organs in the early season
of election years, combined patriotism, image-making, and
criticism of the government but contained few specific policies for the future. Democrats had to look ultimately to their
legislators for serious policy formulation.

Much of it was hardly to be taken seriously. Economic policy provides a case in point. Despite serious reservations
about the workings of business and finance in the war, the
national Democratic platform of 1864 would be silent on

economic policy. One reason, no doubt, was that disagreements within the party over soft and hard money would only complicate an already mortal problem of party unity. But the Democrats cannot be said really to have attempted policy formulation in Pennsylvania, for example. In its place, they offered only short-term exploitation of partisan advantages.

Democrats in Pennsylvania's state house introduced a resolution in the early spring of 1864 urging that the state's U.S. senators be instructed to vote for a bill to pay soldiers in gold rather than in depreciating greenbacks. They were desperate for issues to make them appear the friends of the soldier, having been battered by Republicans for opposing measures giving Pennsylvania's soldiers the right to vote in the field in the next election. But any such payment policy would quickly have bankrupted the United States government and caused financial collapse and, ultimately, military defeat. Republicans pointed that out, though Democrats probably knew it anyhow.[38]

WHILE THE DEMOCRATIC press systematically exploited the race issue and otherwise flailed about wildly, the role the party should have played in policing the Republican administration was accepted by others. In the case of corruption in government contracts, the key initiatives came from a Republican committee of the House of Representatives and from a War Democrat who hated Copperheads and supported Lincoln over McClellan in 1864. There were major investigations and exposés of government connections with business in arms procurement, but these came not from the watchdog opposition party but from the

Contracts Committee of the House. The chair, Republican Charles Van Wyck, whose name appeared on the widely circulated report of the committee in 1863, in fact neglected his work on it to raise a regiment in New York, and the driving force was his fellow Republican, Henry Dawes of Massachusetts. The committee played a role in banishing Simon Cameron from the cabinet, exposed extravagance and conflict of interest in purchases of ships for the Union navy, and damaged John C. Fremont's reputation as administrator of the Western Department.[39] The Democratic New York *World* described the Van Wyck revelations on March 9, 1863. Likewise, internal audits from the Treasury Department uncovered frauds in the New York Custom House, as we have seen in Chapter 1. The Democratic press in New York eagerly seized on that news as well, but Republicans had exposed them.[40]

A War Democrat who opposed McClellan's election in 1864 popularized the image of administration corruption in distributing contracts for military supplies. Henry Morford's *The Days of Shoddy: A Novel of the Great Rebellion in 1861,* published at the end of 1863, is a work too much neglected by historians. Morford was a clerk in the court of common pleas in New York City and dedicated his long and didactic book to the court's Democratic judges who "during the three years of war for the union . . . have not only kept spotless the judicial ermine, but discountenanced all disloyal practices and held the golden mean of patriotic conservatism, the true democracy." Morford found it necessary to apologize in his preface for "the large aggregate of denunciation of national vices, with so small a portion of pointed personalities" to be found in his book. But he hated the "continued and unendurable swindles" symbolized by the new meaning for the word "shoddy," once a term for reused wool but during the war a name for flimsy goods corruptly passed off on government contracts for supplies.[41]

In other words, a War Democrat and ultimate Lincoln supporter and not the opposition essentially coined the term "shoddy" in its modern meaning and greatly popularized its circulation as a general denunciation of the corruption of war industry. Democrats eagerly picked up the term and commonly referred to the Republican party as "shoddyites," but the pioneering work on this was not their own.

THE FOUNDING OF a journal of opinion for an opposition party might be taken as validation of the two-party-system theory of Civil War politics. It would stand as a landmark of reasoned and reasonable opposition. The Democrats had been without such a journal since 1859, when the old *Democratic Review* finally went out of existence. It had been founded back in 1837 in the heyday of Jacksonian democracy. Indeed, in that era of relatively stable competition between Democrats and Whigs, each major party for a time could point to a journal of opinion; the Whigs founded their *American Review* in 1845.[42]

Though no Republican journal of opinion had as yet appeared during the Civil War, Republican dominance of such periodicals as *The Atlantic Monthly* made conspicuous the Democratic void in matching regular, intelligent, and articulate serial publication. It is a sign that the political times were out of joint during the Civil War that the opposition journal of opinion established in 1863 proved to be the notorious *Old Guard*. This monthly, which offered a handsome steel engraving of a different party hero as the frontispiece of

each issue and physically resembled other distinguished serial publications of the era, was the handiwork of C.
Chauncey Burr, a scribbler with a past as checkered as
George Wilkes's. He had once been an antislavery advocate
and a Universalist preacher of some sort, but by the Civil
War he had become a convinced and obsessive white supremacist. He had acted as a publicist for the Spanish dancer
Lola Montez, and his first wife sued him for divorce, apparently because he married someone else.[43]

Burr was a fanatic, and the party heroes featured in his
magazine were most often extremist martyrs to military arrest by the Lincoln administration. Those with the broadest
following depicted in the 1864 election year, for example,
were the peace Democrats Thomas Seymour of Connecticut
and George Pendleton of Ohio. Burr seemed naturally drawn
to the explosive politics of the early republic and featured articles on them in the election year.[44] He shared with the patriotic Henry Morford a detestation of the "Shoddyocracy."[45]
The prose in this monthly journal of opinion was spiced
with Burr's demented poetry, for example, "Cooking the Hell
Broth," based on the witches' scene in *Macbeth:*

Witch—Stanton.

Double, double, toil and trouble,
Fire burn and cauldron bubble,
Liver of the Parker school, Spleen of preacher, tongue
    of fool,
Socinian's eye and Atheist's heart,
Of any, Brownson's better part;
Or Butler's, for the charm will kill
With poisons which they may instil;

With wine from chalice, foeman's blood,
Sacred bread and preacher's rations,
Life-blood of the States and nation's,
Negro's wool and white man's brains,
To miscegenate our vapid veins,
And cherry cheek and ebon lip,
And slime of love that devils sip,
And make the gruel thick and slab,
In throw the heart of brothel's drab,
Add thereto a Sambo's liver,
Fished from old Charon's sluggish river.[46]

For all its irrationality, Burr's poetry shared with the McClellan-supporting organ of the Pennsylvania Democrats in Harrisburg the fascination with prostitution, the dread of miscegenation, and the hatred of the reforming churches.

THE CONSTITUTION OF the United States left the political opposition no role that it much wanted to play. There was a tremendous disincentive to formulate policy on the burning issues of war and peace because the opposition as a party out of power naturally wanted always to wait as long as possible to see who was winning the war before committing to policies.

The Civil War in particular, whose beginning coincided with that of a presidential administration, robbed the opposition party of its potent southern wing and marooned the Democrats in a sea of Republican-controlled government institutions, state and federal. The result was ample frustration and irrational disaffection, of little benefit to the Union war effort.

6

"*Paroxysms of rage and fear*"

THE REPUBLICAN PARTY AT WAR

DURING WORLD WAR II, it is often said, New Deal liberals made their peace with capitalism. Out of the need for business skills to bring about the prodigious production necessary to win the war came a moderating of Democratic ideology and a triumph of the more conservative wing of the party.[1] Economic production lay at the heart of the American contribution to the Allied victory in World War I as well, so much so that President Woodrow Wilson could call the Great War "a war of resources no less than of men, perhaps even more than of men."[2] To mobilize those resources, Wilson, as Franklin Roosevelt would do later in the century, made concessions to business. The American progressive reformers who had hoped the war would provide opportunity for people to see what planning and government control could accomplish were disappointed at the big role business actually played.[3] The pattern seen in the great wars of the twentieth century, then, was for the "reform" wing of the political party in power to lose to the "business" wing.

In the Civil War, the reverse pattern developed. The "reform" or "radical" or antislavery wing of the Republican party emerged from the war as the preponderant power. As the war progressed, the moral appeal of the party's antislavery position increased in importance and prominence while its economic message shrank into the rhetorical background.[4] There were at least two reasons for these strikingly different patterns in war administration in the different centuries. First, the Civil War, unlike the two World Wars, was by no means a war of resources rather than of men. Although President Lincoln studiously and regularly praised the sacrifices made by the soldiers fighting for the Union cause, he never seemed to feel that the producers behind them needed a similar boost. Economic production was not as important to the North's victory in the Civil War as it was to the Allies' victory in the World Wars, and to the extent that it was a factor, it came about less by government planning and coercion than by the operation of free-market forces.[5] Second, the reform plank of the Republican platform—its opposition to the spread of slavery—defined the party's identity more centrally than did any particular reform identified with the Democrats in 1916 or 1940.

On the surface, the doctrines of political economy otherwise associated with the Republican party made it the right party in the right place for fighting a great war in 1861. Imagine the Democrats in the same place, with their reputation for agrarian values and for Jeffersonian reluctance to interpret the Constitution boldly. It is easier to see the Republicans harnessing the economic and manpower energies necessary for a massive modern war effort. But in fact, this image of Republicans is deceptive. Their voting strength before the war was rural rather than urban, and what told on the hustings was as much their political and moral message as their smokestack issues.[6]

Nevertheless, as Eric Foner has proved in a book of classic stature, there was a broad range of opinion within the prewar Republican party. That spectrum, which he definitively described in *Free Soil, Free Labor, Free Men: The Ideology of the Republican Party before the Civil War,* spanned from conservatives who hated the South for holding back economic legislation desired by northern business and industry to intensely moral antislavery activists concerned to end slavery because of its cruelty to African Americans. It is a pity that Foner's book ends with the onset of the Civil War, because nothing as comprehensive or persuasive exists to describe the Republican party at war.[7] And it is not possible simply to extend Foner's scheme for understanding the antebellum Republicans forward into Lincoln's presidency because the Civil War made much of the original Republican outlook, like its platform, irrelevant.

The party's opposition to the slave power remained relevant, of course, and grew in importance after the border states' affiliation with the Union was assured in late 1862. But the economic outlook of the Republicans did not follow a straight path through the war years. There were two important reasons for that, and neither of them has received much attention from historians heretofore.

First, the war served temporarily to unsettle the Republicans' confidence in capitalism. I use the term "capitalism" advisedly here, rather than the term made popular by Foner, "free labor ideology," for Republicans always retained confidence in "free labor." But "free labor," taken literally, comprised only part of the northern economic system, and that by far the more attractive part in the eyes of the nineteenth century. The war, on the other hand, served occasionally to put the focus on the part of the northern economic system in which Americans had less confidence, finance and capital.

That honestly compensated farmers, laborers, mechanics, tradesmen, and shopkeepers would efficiently drive the economy of the country was as much an article of faith as Foner said it was. That they would leave their farms and shops for the army in numbers enough to save the republic seemed likely, too. But whether financiers, capitalists, bankers, brokers, and speculators would be willing to make the sacrifices necessary to sustain the war effort over time appeared less certain. The more speculative sector of the economy had always been the Achilles heel of the northern economic ideal. Moreover, the war added the fear that the problems of finance in the public sector, made necessary by funding a great war, would prove insuperable in fact or unacceptable in prospect to the moneyed classes; the problem was summed up in questions about the "public credit."

Southerners were so aware of the northern sensitivity on the point of finance that at first that seeming weakness in the northern economic system gave Confederates hope that the South could win the war. One ardent Confederate patriot, for example, wrote a South Carolina newspaper early in 1862 to warn against overconfidence. He counseled southerners to act "upon a conviction that [the war] cannot terminate until Lincoln's term of office expires." He pointed out that the "anticipation of financial anarchy at the North, such as to precipitate popular turbulence, will not be realized so soon as many suppose."[8] And a disappointed newspaperman observed toward the end of the summer of 1862, "It was confidently expected that long before this the Federal Government would have broken down under its enormous burden of debt. Active foreign intervention was reckoned upon with sanguine confidence. Many could not believe that the purpose and end of the abolition party could be much longer hidden from the minds of the shrewd and sordid Yankees who were only reaping loss and suffering from the contest."[9]

The theme was not prevalent in southern discussions of the outcome and duration of the war again until 1864, when, paralleling doubts and fears expressed in the northern press and political speeches, Confederates once again discovered hope that the North would fail because of the collapse of its public credit. "Peace Coming through Bankruptcy," proclaimed a Richmond *Dispatch* headline in the early spring, as, like the capitalists in the North and the wary Lincoln treasury, they watched gold prices rise in New York.[10] Familiar and comforting cultural stereotypes could be indulged in that situation. Richmond newspapermen contrasted the fight for southern freedom against "the money bags of the sordid Yankees" in an article about the plight of public credit in the North.[11]

From time to time the fear haunted Republican morale, too. Money was unheroic stuff in war, and some Republicans came to consider the more economically minded members of their party as a special interest to be appeased and not as the vital heart of their party. The publishing history of the popular pamphlet *Our Burden and Our Strength,* written by David A. Wells and distributed by the New York Loyal Publication Society in 1864, illustrates the point. Wells sought to calm fears about the war debt and to point to the abundant financial resources yet available in the North. When John

Murray Forbes was soliciting contributions for printing Wells's work, he told Edward Atkinson:

> I suggest a separate subscription for this—a great many people will pay for a thing like this which they approve, who will not for our *miscellaneous* publications. I therefore suggest sending copies to Mr. Lee who is great on republication of pamphlets—to D. Sears, Oakes Ames, Sml Hooper, Alley Rice—& then get the Bank & Insurance Presidents . . . & other *semi*-patriotics who want our credit kept up to par. I will cheerfully pay if necessary to make it go, but I think the Hunkers & *material interest* men had better take this up & do it up brown rather than *we radicals!* It must be done one way or t'other.[12]

For all the imagined strength of industrialism and "free labor," Republicans and others knew about the unpredictability of the business cycle and the fickleness of finance. Oliver P. Morton, the excitable Republican governor of Indiana, for example, warned President Lincoln in the autumn of 1862 that the country would be lost in sixty days without significant military progress. True, he said, the country could subsist on legal tender for a while—until Americans lost confidence in it and financial ruin followed. "The system may collapse in a single day," he exclaimed.[13]

Nervousness about finance was not a preoccupation of the Old Northwest alone. Henry L. Dawes of Massachusetts, when he grew discouraged over the inaction and indifference to the Contracts Committee revelations in 1862, told his wife, "The times are exceedingly dark and gloomy. The credit of the country is ruined, its arms impotent, its servants rotten, its ruin inevitable . . . Oh that such a cause should be crucified to an unholy alliance between trifling indifference, utter incompetence and reeking corruption."[14]

Fear of speculation haunted even the War Department and generals in the field. Oregon Senator James W. Nesmith, for example, visited General Ulysses S. Grant in winter quarters in Virginia late in 1864 and told an amusing anecdote that revealed the anxieties of Secretary of War Edwin M. Stanton on the subject. Stanton had intercepted a telegram written by a general in what he took to be a code to avoid detection and summoned Nesmith. "You see," Stanton exclaimed, "I have discovered everything!" Nesmith was bewildered, but Stanton went on to explain, "I'm determined, at all hazards, to intercept every cipher despatch from officers at the front to their friends in the North, to enable them to speculate in the stock-markets upon early information as to the movements of our armies." Nesmith examined the telegram and explained that it was not a cipher but rather the Indian language Chinook and that the general was asking for another barrel of whiskey.[15]

The second reason for deviation from the steady road of confidence in the "free labor" system was that northerners' faith in their economic critique of slavery shrank as evidence of Confederate resistance grew. At first, the image in Republican minds of "regional economic stagnation" and stunted economic growth in the slaveholding South gave northern society abundant confidence in its ability to defeat the Confederacy in the war.[16] Thus, on the eve of the First Battle of Bull Run in July 1861, a writer explained to *Atlantic Monthly* readers the necessary weakness of the army of a slave society:

How can an army like theirs be strong? Its members mostly unaccustomed to steady exertion or precise organization; without mechanic skill or invention; without cash or credit; fettered in their movements by the limited rolling stock of their scanty railways; tethered to their own homes by the fear of insurrection; what element of solid strength have they, to set against these things? In the present state of the world, strong in peace is strong in war. In modern times an army of heroes is useless without facilities for arming, transporting, and feeding it, to say nothing of the more ignoble circumstances of pay. Considerations of simple political economy render it almost impossible for a slaveholding army to be strong collectively, nor do the habits of Southern life usually fit its members to be strong singly.[17]

A month later, in the wake of the Bull Run defeat, prospects began to look different, and the hopefulness invested in capitalism lost some of its luster. Thus, the New York *Tribune* warned against the "Foolishness of Contempt" after the battle, saying that "while the North is persuaded, and very justly, of its great superiority in wealth, in population, and in all national resources over the South," the enemy "may have enough . . . for a good while to come." The editors admitted that "we may overrate their poverty and feebleness."[18]

The most startling realization made by northerners in 1861 and 1862 was that their vaunted economic and numerical superiority did not win the war quickly against the weak slave society of the South. The familiar economic critique of slavery for its inefficiency and backwardness began to ring a little hollow. If emphasized too much, that critique could even prove an embarrassment to the Republican administration. In other words, if slave society was as weak and economically backward as the Republicans had always said it was, then why was the North having so much trouble overcoming the Confederacy in a test of arms?

Naturally, not many Republicans were eager to give voice to such sentiments, but it becomes clear upon reading in chronological sequence a substantial body of northern press opinion that the result of their sobering realization about the slave economy was that the Republicans chose not to emphasize material and economic factors in their explanations of war policy. We have been somewhat blinded to the Republicans' change of heart because such a decline in confidence in their modern economy would seem to run counter to the twentieth-century interpretations of the Civil War as the "first modern war."

They had their doubts at the time, nevertheless. The New York *Evening Post,* for example, stated the lesson of the Peninsular Campaign of 1862 in an article entitled "The South as a War Power": "That the South possesses within herself the positive terms of a war power of high grade is now a demonstrated fact. If she had been a separate nation and assailed by France or England, who can doubt that she would have come off victorious? . . . Slavery, which, by our northern theory, we have always set down as an element of weakness, has been converted by the South into an arm of prodigious strength."[19]

The first illusion to be discarded was what historian David M. Potter has called the "Sparticist complex," the belief that slave insurrection lay just around the corner.[20] To judge by popular publications, it may have been more a preoccupation of intellectuals than the general reading public. The *Atlantic Monthly,* for example, ran articles on Denmark Vesey and on Nat Turner in 1861. Newspapers were silent on the subject or attempted to put to rest speculation about a servile uprising within the Confederacy, outright advocacy of which might have seemed bloodthirsty under the assumptions of the age. Ardently antislavery newspapers led the way in assuring the public that emancipation would not lead to servile insurrection. The New York *Tribune,* for example, let their readers know that emancipation would not cause rebellion, though it would aid the war effort by forcing white southerners to watch their slaves carefully to keep them from running off to freedom.[21]

Next came occasional grudging explanations of slavery's surprising strength. The New York *Evening Post* argued that slavery turned out not to be as weak as previously assumed because northerners had forgotten to take into account the despotism of southern society as well:

> Its irrepressible despotism is not limited by the age or sex of subject. Women replace men in the field, and children are forced to perform the labor of men . . . To do full justice to the weight of the slave element on the side of the South, we should complete the analogy of our example by the supposition that the federal government might not only call a million of men into the field, but in the same breath order their wives and children to supply their places in the factories and carry on without interruption such labor as would most effectually feed the war, and all *without a dollar of*

compensation to master or man, which of itself is one
of the most vital terms of military success.[22]

In other words, comparative population figures were deceptive, and the despotism of slavery made a greater percentage
of the population into workers under duress.

The Democrats noted the changed tone of Republican remarks right away and tweaked them about their inconsistency. A New York opposition paper, for example, said, "The
Tribune steadily represented Slavery as an element of weakness to the South, but now regards it as one of positive and
formidable strength."[23]

For the most part, however, the phenomenon is one proven
by lack of evidence rather than by abundant acknowledg-
ments of surprising southern power, and for obvious reasons of patriotism, intellectual consistency, and morality.
But the president himself offers a valuable example. Lincoln's little lessons on free labor, quoted to great effect by
Foner in illustrating the prewar Republican ideology, were
by the late 1850s so important to him that he offered them in
the most surprising places. For example, as a presidential
hopeful in 1859, Lincoln was invited to address the Wisconsin State Agricultural Society in Milwaukee. A partisan
stump speech was inappropriate to the occasion; so Lincoln
offered instead an answer to the southern argument that
slavery was a positive good. He defended the free labor system, beginning with the labor theory of value and arguing
that in the North few men were fixed in the condition of la-
borer for life. He chose to repeat the arguments, nearly ver-
batim, in his first annual message to Congress, delivered on
December 3, 1861.[24] But thereafter Lincoln left off giving gra-

tuitous lectures to the people on free labor economics. And he seldom emphasized the role of resources and numbers in public statements until military victory was in sight late in 1864.

Besides, as the Democrats sensed in pointing out the Republicans' inconsistency, it was easy by 1862 to accommodate a new realization of the strength of a slave economy because that new idea underwrote emancipation: the stronger slavery looked in a situation of war, the more likely slavery was to become a military target. Reformist Republicans were certainly comfortable with that conclusion, whatever had been their previous statements about slavery. All in all, the Republicans grew quieter about the virtues of political economy in the North.

They chose not to emphasize material and economic factors in their explanations of war policy. The moral triumphed in Republican discourse during the war. Horace Greeley provides a good example. Though a staunch believer in protective tariffs and other Whiggish economic ideas, Greeley was also ardently antislavery. After the Battle of Bull Run, the moral forged well ahead of the material in his assessment of the war, and that was reflected in the book he found time to write while the war progressed. *The American Conflict: A History of the Great Rebellion . . . Intended to Exhibit Its Moral and Political Phases* appeared in two volumes in 1864 and meant what it said in its subtitle. The emphasis was on the moral. When Greeley discussed the relative military advantages enjoyed by the North before the war began, he included, as one of fourteen assets, superior population and—as but a small part of the population factor—a "preponderance" in "Manufacturing, Commerce, Shipping, etc."[25] But he gave these material factors little attention or emphasis.

To be sure, the Republicans accomplished an impressive agenda of economic legislation in Congress during the Civil War, amounting, in one historian's estimation, to a "blueprint for modern America" and, in another assessment, to fulfillment of a "vision."[26] But to examine the party in power is not to see the whole party or the party whole. There is also the party in the electorate and the organization itself.[27] We have seen the organization at work in the New York Custom House. And to glimpse the party's connection with the electorate, we can look beyond the halls of Congress to the appeals that were made locally to voters at election time.

By custom, the president did not himself campaign, and the utility of that custom has rarely been commented on. It served to keep one head cool while many others grew overheated. The difference is apparent in the often hysterical letters Lincoln read in his office and the measured, sometimes humorously dismissive, replies they received from the White House. We have already witnessed the cool response to wild demands for soldiers to put down threatened Democratic insurrection in Illinois or Indiana, and the opportunities to see the difference were only multiplied in the presidential election year of 1864.

Thus, Elihu B. Washburne wrote from Illinois in mid-October 1864 that the state was lost without furloughing Illinois troops to come home to vote. Lincoln endorsed the envelope, before filing, "Stampeded."[28] And Edgar Conkling, an official of the National Union Association in Cincinnati, wrote repeatedly begging for the aid of government detectives to help him prove that General McClellan was "not only a theoretical traitor but a practical one a thousandfold greater than [Benedict] Arnold." Conkling badgered the president with secondhand anecdotes about McClellan's guaranteeing Robert E. Lee's escape across the Potomac River after the Battle of Antietam. Lincoln's response was, simply, nothing.[29]

The presence of the unpredictable turncoat George Francis Train on the campaign trail for the Republicans in 1864 serves as a reminder of the gulf that separated the party's respectable policy statements spoken from Washington and the actual message heard by the voters at home in mass meetings and in the local press.[30] Train stumped central Pennsylvania that fall. On successive nights he addressed "working men of the mountains" and "merchants, capitalists and iron-masters" (in Scranton). At Danville "three acres of workingmen" were present to hear him.[31] He toured iron works and rolling mills by day and gave speeches before the men who worked in them by night. Under these circumstances, the Republican economic message was the major purport of his work.

In Pennsylvania, the protective tariff was never far from anyone's mind when the discussion turned to political economy. On that subject, Train was Pennsylvania Republican-orthodox: he advocated protective tariffs. He relied on projecting an image of "squalor and destitution which the election of free trade candidates would bring upon this iron-fisted population."[32] But that message came bundled with another that was anti-British and anti-Semitic.

In whistle-stop quips and long-winded harangues, Train described the Democratic nominating convention in Chicago as a British plot and a conspiracy of European aristocrats in general to destroy the American republic. In effect, Train's campaign was a throwback to the era of the early republic, with its political emphasis on alleging intrigue of the opposition with foreign powers. He wanted to campaign against Great Britain rather than the Democrats. His inveterate anti-British sentiments were now riding a wave of popularity in the country, because of Great Britain's attitude toward the American rebellion. William Cullen Bryant commented in July of the election summer, for example, on the "growing animosity toward Great Britain."[33]

If Train's slant on Republican ideas seems little more than an extreme version of the more respectable idea that the United States represented the last best hope of earth for republicanism, on close examination it was in fact a demonic version of it. In Train's scheme, the key figure became Democratic organizer August Belmont of New York, whom he described as a tool of the Rothschilds. Some Republicans obviously held these views before Train's train chugged into town. The Harrisburg *Telegraph* spoke of Belmont as "the Jew broker" who would help the European bankers to get the North to pay the Confederacy's war debt.[34] Train's Harrisburg speech was lent respectability in the end by brief closing remarks from a prominent local Methodist pastor.

In Scranton, Train warned against a plot to assume the rebel debt "for the benefit of Englishmen and those two merchants of Iscariot, Belmont and [Judah] Benjamin."[35] At Williamsport he blamed McClellan's nomination on "a cabal of Jews at Chicago." Loud applause and laughter signaled the comfort of the audience with the orator's message.[36] Here the familiar campaigning style of alleging conspiracies against the republic also betrayed the Republicans' lack of confidence in finance. This part of their system seemed weak to some who feared that it could be undermined by British or Jewish intrigue.

Somewhat less pointed was a widely republished humorous imaginary dialogue between Jefferson Davis and August Belmont. Aaron F. Perry of Ohio concocted the dialogue as part of a campaign speech in October 1864. Near the end, Perry included Belmont's explanation of his interest in negotiating an end to the war to the Confederate president:

> Mr. President, it is with me a matter of feeling! It is sentiment! (striking his pockets with emphasis) [loud and continued cheering] . . . You are aware of the liberalizing tendency of practical finance. Gentlemen who spend the better portion of their lives in the upper financial circles learn to rise above the narrowness of special adhesions and local attachments. To us one political party is like another; one country like another; one cause like another—in short, one dollar is like another. To us St. Petersburg, Vienna, Berlin, Paris, London, New York, are all the same.[37]

Perry did not say that Belmont was a Jew, but the stereotype of materialism and lack of national feeling was surely recognizable to his hooting audience.

Anti-Semitism represented the dark side of the Republicans' fears about the imminent collapse of the financial part of their vaunted economy. Train was not its only advocate. The eccentric George Wilkes came more prominently into Republican view again in autumn of 1864 with a series of sensational editorials denouncing the alleged gold conspiracy on Wall Street. He blamed the high price of gold on "outside hoarders and private gold misers"—a combination of "Confederate Jews." They were "mere agents of European Premiers and Bankers." Wilkes sent notes on his views and assurances of his support for Lincoln's reelection in late September to Oliver Spencer "Pet" Halsted, who wrote the president about them, enclosing copies of *Wilkes' Spirit of the Times* with editorials from mid-July on the gold question and the ultimate culprits, "European banking Jews."[38] Such appeals can hardly be adequately epitomized as "free labor" ideology.

This strand of Republican political thought has been substantially lost in historical accounts of Civil War politics, but it was not lost on America's Jewish community. By the end of the 1864 canvass, it was apparently more than some could bear. A Jewish citizen from Baltimore named Wolf sent a long letter to the editor of the New York *Evening Post* decrying the growth of anti-Semitism during the war.[39] "The war now raging," Wolf pointed out, "has developed an intensity of malice that borders upon the darkest days of the Spanish inquisition." Was the war "inaugurated or fostered by Jews exclusively?" he asked. "Is the late democratic party composed entirely of Israelites?"

Wolf remarked on the press's ready identification of blockade runners and refugees as Jewish, though other religions among such people were not noted in the press. He related the rise in anti-Semitism particularly to the war years, and he ultimately blamed the Republican party and the party press for this disturbing development. "Local politicians," he commented, "and even some metropolitan journals, have annunciated the lie that we are cowards, that none of us are in the army, and if so, on the other side." Wolf, who had served as secretary of the Fremont convention, had voted for Lincoln in the end, so he felt especially deeply that "least of all should the dominant party, which claims to be the *avant courier* of truth, give expression to the intolerance sown broadcast."[40]

It was anomalous, as the critic Wolf pointed out, that the party extending freedom to a once despised race in the Civil War should at the same time carelessly burden a minority religion with scornful prejudice. Wolf was right to point out that the two ideas were antagonistic. But the Republican party did not have an ideology of consistent political ideals. It assembled an agglomeration of arguments to particular ends at each canvass. The particular end of the anti-Semitic attack on Great Britain was to arouse voters in Pennsylvania's iron districts against the Democrats. They used other arguments elsewhere.

The style of argument was the same, however—alleging conspiracy among the Democrats to undermine the nation. By 1864 that had become as common as any Republican campaign accusation. What had begun in 1862 in New York and elsewhere as tentative and gingerly worded suggestions of treason had under the pressures of a presidential contest and party competition at full throttle become wild and widespread charges; the very keynote speech of the presidential campaign of 1864 was Seward's "Allies of Treason," as we have seen. The effect of two-party competition—under the strain of war, at least, and in an atmosphere of doubt about the legitimacy of party activity—was to make the parties not more moderate and reasonable in their search for voters but more radical and irrational.

And the Democrats, mainly because of an accident of timing, supplied an actual event that made the Republican conspiracy charges more plausible. In their desire to wait to the last moment possible before nominating a presidential candidate and drafting a platform for the fall campaign in 1864, the Democrats fell short of the fatal moment by just one day. They selected McClellan on August 31, and Atlanta fell to Sherman on September 1.

Had their nominating convention come only a day or two later, the Democrats would have felt the same momentum of military events that others did. And instead of hedging their bets with a war candidate and a peace platform, they would surely have bet on the winning horse and run their war candidate on a war platform. There would have been nowhere else for the peace-oriented Democrats to go anyhow. But in fact the Democrats had to placate the peace wing with what became a notorious characterization of the war as a "failure" and with a call for a cessation of hostilities to be followed by a convention of the states to reestablish Union.

Though not as often commented upon directly at the time or since by historians, the tone of other planks could be characterized as practicing brinksmanship and definitely made the Democrats' loyalty conditional. The fourth plank declared that "the repetition of . . . acts" of military interference in elections in the slaveholding border states "will be held as revolutionary" and would be "resisted with all the means and power under our control." The slogan widely repeated on the hustings was "a fair election or a free fight." The *World* in New York mixed loyal opposition platitudes with old-fashioned threats. "If we are beaten on a fair vote, after free discussion," the editors warned in October 1864, "we shall all, as good citizens, swallow our regrets and submit. But we are very sure that we express the unanimous resolve of the party, when we say that if a fair election is not permitted, if we are overborne by the exercise of unconstitutional authority, we shall *not* submit."[41]

And it has gone unnoticed that the Democratic platform invoked the second amendment to the Constitution. It was only the second time in American history that a national party platform had expressed concern over "interference with and denial of the right of the people to bear arms in their defense."[42] The timing of the first invocation of the amendment did not augur well for its resurrection in the midst of the Civil War. The first party to protest infringement of the "right of the people to keep and bear arms" was the Republicans in 1856, at a time when, as the Whig party platform of 1856 expressed it, "a portion of the country [was] being ravaged by civil war." [43] The North did not need the equivalent of "bleeding Kansas" in 1864.

As it was, McClellan, with the advice of party leaders, attempted to rectify the situation of the peace plank single-handedly by denying that he could run on a platform declaring the war a failure, but by then it was too late. And the spectacle of the presidential candidate disavowing his own platform offered little aid to the Democratic canvass.

The peace plank in the Democratic platform greatly accelerated Republican belief in a conspiracy against the Union among the Democrats. It also increased the chances that voters would find the Republican charge plausible. The heated nature of the resulting canvass was commented on by nearly all observers at the time. The independent Philadelphia *Public Ledger,* for example, noted that "political excitement and partisan feeling are so high that, unless cool judgment is sprinkled over this passion, the contending parties are likely to come into collision at every public assemblage."[44] And the New York *Evening Post,* which had contributed its mite to the phenomenon, reflected afterward, "Those who had the patience to read the newspapers for several weeks before the election" saw "into what paroxysms of rage and fear the intelligent and patriotic writers in them were cast everyday of their lives; how they foamed at the mouth in the heat of their indignation at the multitude of traitors on either side; how they grew livid with an almost hourly panic of military interference or of awful fraud; how they predicted invasion from the frontiers, outbreaks in the cities, and conspiracies all over the western rural districts."[45]

The difference between the competitive presidential atmosphere and the beginnings of competition two years earlier is illustrated by the course of Greeley's New York *Tribune*. When rumors of a conspiracy to lure the states of the Old Northwest to the Confederacy first circulated, the *Tribune* rejected their plausibility. "We hold the great body of Democrats of that section," wrote *Tribune* editors on September 18, 1862, "and especially of Illinois, to be loyal and true men, who will stand or fall with the Union."[46]

When sensational events occurred closer to home, however, the *Tribune* circle turned more fearful. As Union soldiers finally put down the draft riots in New York City on July 17, 1863, James R. Gilmore, a writer, met with Horace Greeley and Henry Gay, *Tribune* editors, in the newspaper's offices and heard from War Democrat Richard Busteed that the riot "was planned and set afoot by Govr Seymour, Fernando Wood, and a small *coterie* of leaders of their stripe; to inaugurate a revolution at the North, and overthrow the present Government." Busteed apparently maintained that he had himself attended the secret meetings, but the Republicans in the *Tribune* office did not trust him fully. Even so, Gilmore avowed to President Lincoln, "We shall take steps at once to get at the bottom of the thing."

There was reason for extreme reaction in the *Tribune*

offices, which had been deliberately set afire by the rioters earlier in the week. Yet there was a chilling ingredient of political calculation in the mix as well. Gilmore was not a *Tribune* employee, and he told the president, "If we can succeed in establishing these things as facts, it will be a death blow to Copperheadism, and we shall bless God for this riot, which will then have fully unmasked our Northern traitors."[47] Gilmore wanted the conspiracy established by more reliable authority than Busteed, so he contacted Judge J. W. Edmunds in Lake George, New York. Edmunds was not regarded as an extreme party man, but he had believed for over two years now in such a conspiracy as the one Gilmore and the *Tribune* editors thought they had uncovered. The judge had attempted to persuade Republican Governor Edwin D. Morgan to organize a home guard in anticipation of the revolt in New York. When Morgan would not be stampeded, Edmunds attempted to organize a home guard without the sanction of the state but found "men of property were not enough awakened to the danger to engage in the movement." Edmunds shared with Gay and Gilmore a desire to prosecute the political leaders of the alleged draft riot conspiracy, but he needed official sanction from the government, at least the authority of a United States district judge. A voluntary inquiry would be a "farce."[48]

Frustrated by the judge's response, Gilmore did not think the U.S. attorney, Delafield Smith, had the weight to make the charges stick, and Gilmore wanted an exposé that would "have such weight with the people as not only to crush the Copperhead leaders, but the party itself." Then "the North [would] once more [be] made a united people—united by the democratic party seeing the depth of treason into which their leaders are plunging them." "The real danger to the

Union lies here," warned Gilmore, in the distorted anti-party vision that belittled the real enemy, Robert E. Lee's army, and magnified the opposition of such men as the cautious and legalistic Seymour.[49]

In the summer of 1864 the *Tribune* reported the "rumor of a North-Western Rebellion . . . floating in the air" and lent credence to the notion that Clement L. Vallandigham, William B. Reed, George H. Pendleton, and George E. Pugh were among a half million disloyal men organized in the Order of American Knights, including "200,000 McClellan minutemen of New York."[50] Two weeks later, the newspaper admitted that the charges seemed exaggerated and backed away from its endorsement.[51] But nothing so fired belief in the chimerical as opposition from the other political party. The *Tribune* did another and final about-face eleven days later, referring to reports from Missouri and from Indiana:

> *The World* has for weeks been ridiculing the accounts of ProSlavery conspiracies and secret societies in the West which meditate a subversive revolution. Yet it knows thoroughly that these conspiracies, these societies, have a real existence, and that their object has been truly exposed. There were errors and exaggerations in some of the details elicited at St. Louis—as we indicated at the time—but the essential facts were truly revealed. Gen. Carrington's expose at Indianapolis was terse, lucid, and within the truth.[52]

As for the Republican officials who compiled and released the government reports that built the image of these now discredited conspiracies, their sincerity has always been difficult to measure. Were they indulging partisan tactics or falling prey to the sincere figments of imaginations fevered by partisan excess? Likely the motives were mixed, but for the most famous of the reports, the case for sincerity of belief is as sound as the case for inaccuracy of content.

The most famous and influential of the lot was Joseph Holt's *Report . . . on the "Order of American Knights."* As the most careful student of these episodes, Frank L. Klement, has pointed out, Holt, the judge advocate general of the army, gave the report he assembled from testimony of various agents to his superior, Secretary of War Edwin M. Stanton, on October 8, 1864, and it was subsequently published in Republican newspapers and by the Union Congressional Committee as the *Report of the Judge Advocate General on the "Order of American Knights," alias "Sons of Liberty": A Western Conspiracy in Aid of the Southern Rebellion.*[53] In retrospect, the report surely seems ridiculous, if the Democratic party constituted a loyal opposition. For example, Holt, who revised downward the estimates given him by others, nevertheless put the figure for Illinois membership in the secret organization to aid the rebellion at 100,000 to 140,000. In the presidential election of 1864, by comparison, McClellan's vote in Illinois numbered only 158,730. Holt's high estimate, in other words, comes close to approximating the number of Democrats in Illinois. Holt's estimate for Indiana was 75,000 to 125,000, and the McClellan vote would total only 130,233 there. Since the judge advocate general was halving the figures he had received from others, in many cases those wildly hysterical estimates of membership had exceeded the total number of Democratic voters in the states. Horace Greeley was a careful student of election returns and published what remains to this day the best source for them, *The Tribune Almanac,* but he did not check the figures against the previous returns, apparently, or think particularly clearly on the subject.

And yet Holt's report was surely not a political scam. The election of 1864, more perhaps than any previous election in recent American history, boiled down to the contest in one state, Pennsylvania, and Pennsylvania was one of the October-voting states. By the time Holt's *Report* was printed and released in the Republican press, election day in the most important state had already passed—as it had in Indiana as well, the state figuring the most prominently in the various allegations of a Northwest conspiracy. To be sure, presidential election days followed in November, but politicians knew that there was no turning around a state after the momentum of October had been reckoned.[54] No calculating politician would have sprung his "October surprise" *after* election day.

The pattern of belief in secret treason in the case of William Cullen Bryant's sober *Evening Post* was similar to that at the *Tribune*. When the reports of a Northwest conspiracy surfaced in the St. Louis *Democrat* in mid-summer 1864, the New York newspaper sniffed at the alarmism of the "country journals" and dismissed the allegations as "greatly exaggerated."[55] But the Democratic platform passed subsequently at Chicago drew the paper's attention, and when Holt's report appeared in October, the *Evening Post* featured it as "highly important."[56] The election in New York was, unlike that in Pennsylvania, not over; and in light of Holt's report, the *Evening Post* became alarmed at the assertion in the Democratic platform of the right to bear arms and asserted the hope that voters "cannot fail, we think, to see that the election of McClellan would be the signal for the destruction of all peace and order in the northern states—the beginning of a frightful and bloody reign of anarchy."[57] The greater the competition in the canvass, the less reasonable grew the message even of the generally reasonable *Evening Post.*

The New York *Times* also became increasingly alarmed, at first saying that they would "require a great deal more evidence" to believe the allegations about secret treasonous societies in the Northwest than had been revealed in the early summer.[58] But after the Democratic convention met in late August, the *Times* warned against a Democratic plot to reconstruct the Union with New England left out.[59]

A simpler universe of stark choices characterized many areas outside the metropolis. At a Washington's birthday banquet in Harrisburg, Pennsylvania, the editor of the local Republican newspaper responded to a call for a toast to the loyal press with these words, "Every journalist in the land was either a sentinel in the service of freedom, or a tory in the employ of treason."[60] In the legislature, Republicans made their point with a resolution demanding that all Pennsylvanians requesting claims for damages arising from the recent Confederate raid on Chambersburg must first prove their loyalty; Chambersburg and the counties through which the Confederate raid passed traditionally voted Democratic.[61] The Harrisburg Republicans expressed none of the big city editors' initial skepticism about the Northwest conspiracy.[62]

Harrisburg's Republicans believed in the *Appeal of the National Union Committee to the People of the States,* one of the standard Republican documents of the campaign, which warned that "in the West armed preparations have already been made . . . to follow the example of the South."[63] These documents were not distributed to individuals but in packages of one thousand copies to organizations, which had only to pay the freight to receive them.[64]

In the Old Northwest itself, skepticism was quickly dispersed and major emphasis was placed on the threat of armed conspiracy. The Chicago *Tribune,* beginning in late July, gave full and repeated coverage to allegations of a great Northwest conspiracy. To those who would say "But these plots—this secret society business, is getting to be an old story; is about played out," the *Tribune* replied repeatedly that the southern rebellion itself "was fledged and nursed into strength by just this method."[65]

SOME HISTORIANS believe that, with "the Union and the Constitution in the balance, wartime elections restored in the public mind an appreciation of the importance of party competition for republican government."[66] Of course, the Democrats, in their disadvantaged position, had never lost that belief, but for their part, the Republicans did not necessarily come away from the elections of 1864 with that lesson. Even President Lincoln's conciliatory post-election message, quoted at the beginning of this book, stopped short of an endorsement of a two-party system in wartime. His statement did not contain a single one of the customary justifications of a loyal opposition. Lincoln believed that the election had "demonstrated that a people's government can sustain a national election, in the midst of a great civil war." Otherwise, the best he could say for the experience was, "Let us . . . study the incidents of this, as philosophy to learn wisdom from, and not . . . as wrongs to be revenged."[67]

Lincoln knew his party colleagues well, and revenge was very much on some Republicans' minds. After Lincoln's reelection there was no more consensus on the operation of a two-party system in wartime than there had been at the beginning of the war. The editors of the Harrisburg *Telegraph*, for example, complained of Lincoln's "leniency in hesitating to treat the traitors of the North with a proper spirit of severity. He has forborne to recognize the unarmed as culpable as the armed traitors."[68] "Give the Screws Another Turn" was the sentiment of the Pennsylvanians, who urged people to "insist that President Lincoln treat these aiders and comforters of the enemy [such as the Philadelphia *Age*, a Democratic newspaper] just as Gen. [Andrew] Jackson would have done, and as Gen. Butler has done."[69] Like the Federalists after the War of 1812, said the Pennsylvania Republicans in late November,

> as we become victorious over treason and rebellion, will the party in our midst, which sought to give aid and comfort to the conspiracy, *pass out of existence*. Peace could not be established otherwise. There could be no security for the honor and glory of the Government, if its worst enemies were allowed to exist in their very midst unrebuked and unpunished . . . Both [rebellion and the Democratic party] must . . . pass out of existence, in order to render the Union secure and the Government pure for all time to come.[70]

Other sentiments of revenge appeared after the election. Senator Charles Sumner of Massachusetts, who did not harbor sentiments of revenge against the South and later argued against hanging Civil War battle paintings in the Capital because they showed some Americans victorious over others, did not feel the same charity toward the northern Democrats. It was reported in the press that after the election Sumner proclaimed the Democratic party dead, "now buried where it could never be reached again. Loathsome and putrid from corruption, it had been a nuisance while it was above ground . . . The Democratic party had ceased to be loyal. It was no longer patriotic . . . It should no longer exist."[71]

Salmon P. Chase urged in November that the government should now go after the defeated Democratic candidate, McClellan, and investigate him officially for his military failures on the Peninsula two years earlier: "I have long thought that the whole action of General McClellan should be made the subject of a thorough enquiry by an impartial & thoroughly competent Board or Court. His acts on several occasions it seemed to me at the time, if not prompted by evil design, were of such fatal consequence that an investigation was imperatively demanded. If they endure the ordeal of fair scrutiny I shall rejoice; for no honest American can wish ill to any man who has been in the country's service."[72]

The election of 1864 by no means convinced Chase that the opposition to the Republicans had been loyal and legitimate. He wrote the postmaster general this letter less than a week after the election: "We have been on the brink of civil war in the North. Nothing but divided counsels of opposition leaders saved us from it. The strength & ramifications of the conspiracy, now being exposed at Indianapolis, of which the recent attempts at St. Albans, Sandusky, Chicago, & . . . other places were parts are frightful. It is now effectively suppressed by the activity of the Government and the voice of the people in the elections."[73]

In general, Republicans took the view after 1864 that an opposition may be necessary or inevitable in a republic in peacetime but not in a war for the Union, and that the Democratic party would disappear and parties would be reorganized entirely around new issues after the war was over. The Chicago *Tribune,* for example, predicted that "there will be parties hereafter as heretofore. There will be divisions of sentiment on questions of public policy and vigorous animosities, and stout contests at the polls, but not as on Tuesday last, for a decision as to whether the nation shall die or live."[74] Later, the *Tribune* editors took issue with "Copperhead papers which refuse to bow to the verdict of the people upon the questions at issue in the last election" and "allege as their apology the necessity of an opposition party." The *Tribune* pointed out that "a wholly new opposition party will be formed."[75]

Lincoln's victory reminded editors of the New York *Times* of the reelection of James Monroe and the ensuing "era of good feelings," a period in American history without two-party competition. They recalled the words of John C. Calhoun in 1814, defining a "factious opposition" as one that "sickens at the sight of the prosperity and success of the country."[76] They realized by late November, however, that

> an opposition is almost as necessary in a constitutional State, as an Administration, and the fault we have found with the Democrats was not that they constituted an opposition, but that their opposition was of the kind it was.
>
> It is not, therefore, merely because they found fault, that the Democrats brought themselves to ruin and confusion, but because they did nothing but find fault; not because they were in opposition, but because they opposed everything the Government did or proposed to do—good, bad

and indifferent. Opposition of this kind is what is called factious, and when carried on in time of war, inures to the benefit, not of the country, but of the public enemy.[77]

The *Times* thought *an* opposition was a good thing, perhaps, but not *the* opposition the Republicans actually faced in the Civil War. Whether any actual opposition could live up to their ideal remains a question. In other words, the position often expressed by Republicans after the election of 1864 was that a loyal opposition may be a necessity but that the Democratic party was not a loyal opposition and either had been destroyed in the recent elections or would disappear before 1868. The Philadelphia *Inquirer* echoed the *Times*'s view that the aftermath of the election seemed "as if a 'new era of good feeling' had already spread its benignant wings over the land."[78]

The Republicans did not learn in 1864 to appreciate "the importance of party competition for republican government" in wartime.

IN *FOUNDING BROTHERS*: *The Revolutionary Generation*, the historian Joseph Ellis has characterized the politics of the 1790s as "a truly cacophonous affair." "In terms of shrill accusatory rhetoric, flamboyant displays of ideological intransigence, intense personal rivalries, and hyperbolic claims of imminent catastrophe," he says, "it has no equal in American history."[79] But that era met its match in the tone of Civil War politics—and for the same underlying reason. Americans were returned in the 1860s to the style of political catastrophism and ideological extremism associated with politics in the early republic, when there was no firm conception of a loyal opposition. Rebellion brought the old assumptions about opposition to the fore again. Both eras were times when, to use Ellis's words describing the earlier period, "neither side possessed the verbal or mental capacity to regard the other as anything but treasonable."[80]

7

The Civil War and the Two-Party System
A RECONSIDERATION

ALTHOUGH THIS BOOK has been organized chronologically as much as possible and has included anecdotes documenting the daring behavior of America's Civil War politicians, it is, like all history, ultimately an argument. Each chapter is meant to prove that the two-party system was not a decisive factor in bringing military victory to the North. Let us see the argument whole now.

Only to a degree had Americans internalized the two-party system on the eve of Civil War, and not many people thought parties should operate during a rebellion or invasion. In the immediate wake of the fall of Fort Sumter, Democrats and Republicans alike voiced hopes that party issues would be forgotten at least until the rebellion was quelled. There was much hypocrisy and self-interested manipulation of the sentiment against party, but even so, there was also more sincere belief than the current literature on the "political nation" and "partisan imperative" would allow: for this we have, as opposed to words only, *behavioral* evidence, most conspicuously, the actions of Hiram Barney, Collector of the Custom House in New York.[1]

Americans had, on the other hand, substantially internalized the Constitution, at least the shape of government laid out in it and notably the provisions for elections for Congress every two years and for president every four. This inexorable election clock, which Roy F. Nichols first called to our attention years ago and which has still to be appreciated fully by historians, collided with the anti-party sentiment evoked by the war. Americans would have elections without fail, but in the midst of a great rebellion they felt uneasy with the organization of an opposition party to contest those elections. The shock that came when politicians obeyed old habits of organization and campaiging in 1862–1863 reached dimensions just short of violent behavior: conspicuously, in the publication of threatening resolutions from Illinois troops in winter quarters, disillusioned with the organization of opposition in the Illinois legislature beginning in January 1863.

The rise in 1863 of what the historian George M. Fredrickson identified a generation ago as "the doctrine of loyalty," advertised and institutionalized by organizations like the Loyal Publication Society and the Union Leagues, was in part a response to that return of genuinely competitive politics.[2] It was not a gratuitous assertion of authority by displaced New England elites nor a mere tactic for the election of 1864. In a context of loyalty and disloyalty, a return to normal political competition constantly threatened violence. In the East as in the Old Northwest, the conventional rough-and-ready tactics of partisan maneuver could lead to the taking up of arms. Simon Cameron, for example, had a long-standing reputation for stealing elections, but when Pennsylvania Republicans called on his talents once again in 1863, his customary operating methods were not deemed a matter of political high jinks but brought the en-forcement of discipline in the Democratic party with fire-arms and provoked various proposals to use military means to gain political power.

The politicians in the North also returned to their time-tested practice of imagining conspiracies and then cam-paigning against them. As the historian Michael F. Holt has argued, success for such campaigns depended on the exist-ence of real events that could be woven into a believable con-spiratorial pattern. The political history of the period ap-pears to modern eye to lack any such pattern of real events. But we forget that during the war the assumption that par-ties should not operate as they did in peacetime transformed the customary organization for elections into a seeming sign of sedition. Thus we can apply the same analogy that histo-rian George C. Rable pointed to in the history of the Confed-eracy: the similarity of the extremist politics of the early re-public to those of the Civil War. Both periods of political history were distinguished by widespread inability to com-prehend a legitimate role for an opposition party.[3] Besides, in the North, the example of secession itself, inevitably asso-ciated in partisan minds with the Democratic party, took its place as yet another event in the pattern of Democratic con-spiracy.

The continuing thralldom of the press to the two-party sys-tem held it back from performing crucial roles we associate with modern party politics in wartime. The pre-professional journalism of the era failed the parties, the public, and the soldiers themselves in its analysis of war. The Bull Run de-feat in July 1861 and the next summer's trauma of the defeat of McClellan's grande armee on the Virginia Peninsula elic-ited from the press a heroic critique of strategy, entrenchment, and fortification that kept popular and political analysis from perceiving war's future direction. Instead, even President Lincoln, though clear-headed about military professionalism and free of bias against Democratic generals, absorbed from the devastating and sustained criticism of McClellan's generalship a suspicion of "strategy" and a preference for what Lincoln called hard desperate fighting. The New York *World,* a close ally of McClellan in 1864, briefly formulated as a Democratic response an analysis of Civil War strategy that was forward-looking, but it died aborning with the failure of the presidential campaign for the candidate the doctrine was tailored to defend.

By the summer of 1864 "strategy" had become a Republican bugbear, and it was by no means clear that the administration thought of itself as "organizing" victory. It is not as easy as it may appear in the history books to link the administration genealogically with other forward-looking military techniques and attitudes often said to have been legacies of the American Civil War. In substantial part, the reason lay in the retrograde and misinformed interpretation of the war formulated by the politicians and their partisans in the press, as Bruce Tap and Eric T. Dean have shown. The two-party system, of which, as historian Michael Schudson points out, the press was but a junior branch, bore responsibility for this dysfunctional analysis of Civil War military strategy in public political debate.

The partisan nature of the mid-century press also made journalists themselves adversaries of freedom of the press in wartime. Party competition inhibited the professionalization of the press, and Civil War journalism made few approaches to its modern institutional position as a fourth-estate watchdog on the government. It is difficult to conceive of a role more important for a party system in wartime than the preservation of domestic civil liberties, but in the area of press freedom, conspicuously, the party system in fact threatened rather than protected freedom of speech.

When it came to ideas rather than behavior, the record of the Civil War press—and by extension of the parties that manipulated the press—was more dismal. Republican journalists instigated the suppression of rival newspapers only occasionally. But they were nearly always available to explain and rationalize interference with the press taken on the initiative of others—from thickheaded generals like Ambrose Burnside to frightened administration officials in Washington.

The loyal opposition in the North during the Civil War remains to this day in crying need of analysis. To the historian Eric McKitrick, its role seemed too obvious to bother to describe, but to politicians in the Civil War, its role was not clear at all. Assessing the evidence from a modern perspective, one must conclude that the U.S. Constitution left the opposition party very little role, especially in a war begun early in the term of a president who had the makings of a determined commander-in-chief. When the lesson of the country's unwritten constitution that parties cannot oppose wars fundamentally—one of the principal legacies of the first American party system—was applied to the present conflict, the opposition faced years of powerless frustration. Instead of closing ranks and putting aside internal differences to unite for victory in the election that lay in the remote future, the Democrats during the Civil War indulged in poisonous criticism of the country and lapsed into suicidal factionalism, to this day not satisfactorily explained by historians.

The Republican party did not follow a moderate course either, despite the demands put on its organizational abilities and ideals by an unprecedentedly great war and by the surprising level of resistance mustered by the Confederate States of America. In the end, the radical antislavery wing of the party triumphed over the more conservative wing interested in economic growth—a phenomenon difficult to explain by the customary dynamics of the two-party system or by a conventional understanding of the nature of Union victory as a matter of resources, industrial production, and numbers. To be sure, factionalism in the Repubican party—given its predominance in the Congress and in the states throughout the North—is more easily understood than factionalism in the Democatic party. The dominant "in's" had more occasion for infighting than the desperate "out's." It is a tribute to the antislavery idealism of the Republican party that it did not moderate its policies in line with Democratic criticism and seek compromise with the slave power. Instead, Republicans ignored the Democrats entirely, spurned compromise and concession, and sought emancipation instead of mere containment of slavery.

Put to a trying test in a presidential election in the midst of the rebellion in 1864, the Republicans obeyed habit and campaigned with the customary accusations of conspiracy against the opposition—now documented in thick government reports on allegedly disloyal organizations in the North. When it was all over, despite admonitions from their president and party leader Abraham Lincoln not to entertain thoughts of revenge but to learn lessons for the future from the bitterly fought contest, many Republicans persisted in their doubts about the legitimacy of the opposition party they actually faced during the Civil War, the Democratic party. They did not take a lighthearted view of an opposition party that to them harbored traitors in its midst, and instead, the Republicans often assumed that the Democratic party, now discredited by the people in the election, would likely disappear and bring, if not a new era of good feelings, then a reorganization of parties for the new era to follow in peacetime.

IT IS CERTAINLY possible to believe that "the North had a decisive advantage over the South because it continued to have a two-party rivalry during the war" even after reading the assessment of Civil War politics laid out in the previous chapters of this book. But surely believing in that advantage is no longer as easy a matter—not one on which there should be consensus and little debate. Yet that is substantially the state of interpretation of Civil War politics at this moment. To survey what historians of northern politics have said on the subject over the last generation is to discover a glacial unanimity that has virtually frozen scholarship and fresh investigation of the subject.

Remarkably, this reigning paradigm of interpretation of northern politics in the Civil War began as little more than an aside in a scholarly paper about Jefferson Davis read at a conference at Gettysburg College in 1958. After contrasting the Confederate president's leadership qualities with Abraham Lincoln's at considerable length, the great historian David M. Potter threw out at the very end of his paper "another suggestion that comes to mind. This is the possibility that the Confederacy may have suffered real and direct damage from the fact that its political organization lacked a two-party system."[4]

Hailing Potter's comment as "the most original single idea to emerge from the mass of writing that has been done on the Civil War in many years,"[5] the historian Eric McKitrick expanded it in an essay that is itself now viewed as "brilliant"—"one of the most stimulating analyses of Civil War politics ever written."[6]

Today, Potter's idea has been comfortably absorbed into the basic synthesis of Civil war scholarship. In one of his masterful summations of Civil War history, for example, James M. McPherson introduced the theory this way: "A vital difference in the structure of Union and Confederate politics tempered Northern divisiveness: the North had political parties, the South did not. The absence of parties in the South paradoxically produced an opposition that became unmanageable precisely *because* it was non-partisan. Without the institution of parties, the opposition became personal, factional, and sometimes irresponsible."[7]

McPherson repeated his endorsement of the idea in his influential book *Battle Cry of Freedom,* identifying "the absence of parties" as "a source of weakness" in the Confederacy. "In the North," he asserted, "the two-party system disciplined and channeled political activity," making the "Republican party . . . the means for mobilizing war resources."[8] And Phillip S. Paludan, in his volume on northern society during the war written for the prestigious New American Nation series, put it this way: "The Union had a political vitality and coherence the Confederacy lacked. Northern political parties kept dissent within limits and were rallying points for patronage. They organized divergent viewpoints into effective platforms." Political "turmoil" in the North, he concluded, "strengthened the government."[9]

The two-party-system theory has found its way into the standard constitutional history textbook as well, despite the fact that the U.S. Constitution made no provision for political parties. The "continuous operation of political parties in the North" during the Civil War, say Alfred H. Kelly, Winfred A. Harbison, and Herman Belz, "throws light on the Union's ultimate success":

> Party organization was a means by which federal authorities mobilized and sustained popular energies in support of the war. Moreover, party loyalties restrained states'-rights tendencies and brought federal and state governments into closer harmony, in contrast to the partyless South where states' rights impeded the Confederate war effort. Risky though elections were, especially with opponents of the war involved, they were important in focusing and reinforcing northern popular attitudes toward the war.[10]

Historians have been swept off their feet by the idea. It does sound simple, and yet the idea is counter-intuitive or "paradoxical," as McPherson said. Presumably that counter-intuitive quality accounts for the failure of the two-party-system theory to emerge as a way of explaining northern victory in the Civil War until almost a hundred years after the war's conclusion. But after the long wait, the idea now tyrannizes our understanding of Civil War politics, being held up, in the most recent survey of the literature in the field, as a "stunningly imaginative," "original," and "breathtakingly ingenious" model.[11]

AND YET TIME has not been kind to the once secure historical assumptions on which the two-party-system theory was based. Two assumptions were of crucial importance. First, the theory relied on a sharp contrast between the poor performance of the Confederacy—which was without political parties—and Union victory, political parties and all. David Potter had come up with the idea as an alternative explanation for Confederate defeat, more satisfactory from the standpoint of social science than his comparison of the leadership qualities of Lincoln and Davis as individuals. At bottom, then, lay the assumption that the defeat of the Confederacy was a matter of internal collapse, preventable by better leadership or a better political system. But the idea that the Confederacy collapsed through internal disunity, a theory first suggested by Frank Owsley's *State Rights in the Confederacy* in 1925, is no longer universally accepted. Gary Gallagher and other new historians of the Confederacy, like William Blair and George C. Rable, have challenged the idea decisively.[12]

A second and more important assumption for evaluating northern politics was that two-party systems bred unity rather than disunity in the nation. That notion formed part of the fundamental parliamentary critique of totalitarianism and emerged strongly from the Second World War to develop into a conviction that parties actually had a moderating effect on political differences.[13] But that assumption, whatever its validity for twentieth-century polities, has been called into question by new interpretations of the nineteenth-century American political system. The "republican thesis," which emerged in American historical writing after Potter and McKitrick wrote about the Civil War and the two-party system, argued that American political parties operated most effectively by arousing the electorate to crusades against imaginary conspiracies with sinister designs to destroy the republic. Politicians conventionally relied on creating irrational monsters against which to rally the people into mortal political battle to save the republic. In other words, American politics operated most effectively by heating up the political atmosphere and not by cooling it down and moderating extremes.[14]

Looking back on the two-party-system theory of Civil War politics a generation later, we are apt to find it a little difficult to pin down precisely. After all, Potter mentioned it only as an aside and never himself returned to examine the idea closely. McKitrick's later explanation of the idea came at article length only. At that, the article was diffuse in form and, as even one of its greatest admirers puts it, "idiosyncratic."[15] Examined closely more than thirty years later, McKitrick's argument identified four advantages of a two-party system to the North's war effort. The first advantage lay in forming a government and cultivating and bringing forth political talent. The second came in its ability to smooth federal-state relations—that is, to restrain states' rights tendencies, as the constitutional historians explained the point later. Third, the two-party system created an ultimately identifiable, responsible, and loyal opposition, an opposition that was "manageable," as McPherson put it later. Fourth, the party system constituted "a vehicle of communication," a way of focusing and reinforcing public opinion and organizing effective platforms.

To this day, some of the points seem irrefutable. Government formation in the Confederacy, for example—by balancing geographical origins in cabinet selections more than factions within a ruling party—produced advisers and department heads for Jefferson Davis who were inferior to those selected by Abraham Lincoln. The remaining points, however, seem less compelling now. Let us examine the second point about smoothing federal-state relations. McKitrick here contrasted the northern experience of smooth organization with the problems of states' rights in the Confederacy, to which Owsley had called attention. But the idea of internal collapse in the Confederacy has suffered in recent years, as we now know. It is true that Richmond's relations with Georgia and North Carolina offered Davis more flash points of conflict and irritating frictions than relations with most of the states of the North offered Lincoln. But *most* of the states of the Confederacy did not offer Davis much trouble either.[16]

Focusing on the North, we can see that Lincoln's relations with states across the Union were facilitated not by two-party competition but by one-party dominance. So important was this one-party domination to state-federal cooperation that Republican governors in two states, Illinois and Indiana, extended Republican control by eliminating effective party competition from government, out of worry that Democrats would interfere with the war effort. Richard Yates and Oliver P. Morton managed to dissolve their legislatures once Democrats gained control of them. The lesson of the Old Northwest, then, was precisely the opposite of that posited by the two-party-system theory.[17] It might even be argued from the examples of the Old Northwest that a too-vigorous operation of party competition under the strains of a great war proved insupportable to harried administrators and occasionally threatened republican government itself.

On that same point, McKitrick also underestimated the difficulties posed to the Lincoln administration in the eastern states that elected Democratic governors in the course of the war. The potential for violent confrontation was more evident in New York in the draft riots and their aftermath in

1863 and in the suppression of the New York *World* and *Journal of Commerce* in 1864. The politicians' penchant for brinksmanship was always dangerous in such situations and made it easy for S. L. M. Barlow to envision violent conflict with federal authorities or Manton Marble to risk it willingly for the sake of partisan advantage.

Those near-conflicts between state and federal governments help us to put into properly nerve-wracking context the well-known friction between Governor Seymour and President Lincoln over New York's draft quotas in the wake of the draft riots in 1863. Seymour's contentious correspondence with the administration in Washington reminds us of the importance of one-party dominance to smooth federal-state relations. After all, the Empire State held some 20 percent of the North's population, as the historian Eugene C. Murdock aptly points out, and the breakdown of negotiations over draft quotas between the Lincoln administration and the New York governor in August 1863 was potentially problematic for the Union war effort.[18] Because New York and Washington could not reach agreement, despite a voluminous and niggling correspondence on the subject, the War Department felt compelled to station 10,000 troops and three batteries of artillery in New York for the draft. That number was from all evidence greater than the number actually brought into the army from New York by conscription in the summer 1863 draft.[19] The point here is not that Democrats proved disloyal when in power and directly and maliciously hindered the war effort. The point is that political competition did not *help,* let alone afford some "decisive" advantage to the North.

Before examining the central point about a manageable and loyal opposition, let us look at McKitrick's fourth point, his conception of the party system as "a vehicle of communi-cation." An institutional analysis of the nineteenth-century American press reveals the problems of any such simple as-sertion. The system was not *a* vehicle of communication. Each party and its noisy newspapers constituted *vehicles* of communication with very different messages for the north-ern people.

One hears few echoes of the strident rhetoric of Civil War politics in the pages of McKitrick's analysis of the two-party system. Instead, his characterizations of party debate in the North dwelt on the obligation of party opposition to pro-vide "clear substitute[s] for policies . . . [they] denigrated."[20] He spoke of "refinement and precision" lent "to the issues" by wartime elections and of "continual affirmation and reaffirmation of purpose."[21] McKitrick's analysis contained none of the language that most American historians would soon come to use to describe the political persuasions of this period: "paranoid style," "conspiracy . . . and deceit," "images of counter-subversion," "apocalyptic sense," and "crusading against antirepublican monsters."[22] Such discourse was not intended to lead to consensus and moderation and most likely led in the opposite direction. It did not constitute "communication" in the positive sense, though it was aw-fully effective in spreading fear.

When it came to the crucial point—the third identified above—McKitrick asserted that there was "certainly no need here to discuss the beneficial functions of a 'loyal opposi-tion.'" Yet many during the Civil War did not take those functions for granted, and the supposed advantages were a long time gaining acknowledgment by historians in the twentieth century.[23] We *do* need to discuss the idea of a loyal opposition in war as it was understood by the Civil War generation, because their understanding was different from ours and affected their behavior.

A major impediment to recovering their mindset lies in our modern-day reliance on the outlook of social science. People in the Civil War era did not have social science to tell them that the Republican party and the Democratic party—which we know only from hindsight emerged intact from the four-party chaos of 1860—constituted a "system." I have been unable to find anyone during the Civil War—not the politicians themselves, not the newspaper editors who commented on the parties' activities daily, nor any intellectual observing political developments with more detachment—who used the term "system" in connection with the parties in America. We owe that idea to the later abstractions of social science. For Americans in the middle of the nineteenth century, there was no two-party system. Their conceptual framework for interpreting politics predated the dawn of social science by a generation at least, and that made the idea that good consequences for the nation could flow from the indulgence of selfish ambition for office and eager fault-finding difficult to swallow. The intellectual justification for a two-party system—which was piecemeal and incomplete on the eve of the Civil War—simply defied the moralistic way most people in that era thought about the world around them.

The insight of the historian Gordon Wood is crucial. As he has pointed out, nineteenth-century Americans owed to their eighteenth-century ancestors a way of looking at the world that they thought rational.[24] They had difficulty imagining that good consequences were likely to flow from bad intentions—and vice versa. Political economy, with its assumption that economic efficiency was derived from personal pursuit of selfish interest, seemed a "dismal" science, and such reasoning was narrowly confined to economic thinkers. Moreover, Americans preferred a more cheerful version of economics emphasizing the creative powers of free labor.[25] *The Federalist* had also suggested that "ambition must be made to counteract ambition" in explaining the founders' solution to the problems of faction or party, but their heirs in the middle of the nineteenth century took from them their anti-party spirit rather than their sober view of human nature in politics.[26] Most thinkers believed that historical events were definitely the consequence of individual intentions, again as Gordon Wood has pointed out, and they resisted ideas of impersonal social forces or an irresistible tide of history.[27]

The persistence of such a pre-modern outlook made a two-party system difficult to understand in wartime. Its consequences for government did not flow from good intentions. They came from ambition for office, and at bottom many people knew it. Thus a two-party system proved at best a puzzling anomaly or a troubling presence in a virtuous republic; at worst it was a social evil.

There remains, after all, a crucial need to discuss the idea of a loyal opposition during the Civil War because there was, in the eyes of the people at the time, no two-party "system" to preserve. There was only this party or that one. The reluctance of many in the era to accept the idea of a loyal opposition in the crisis caused them to mistake ordinary political organization and opposition for sedition rather than the normal operation of a tried-and-true "system." Republicans did not need, under the circumstances of a war for the Union, much evidence to reach a sinister and conspiratorial conclusion: bad results—the unexpectedly stubborn and continued and bloodying resistance of the slave power—

must have been the consequence of evil political intentions within the North, cloaked in the conspiracies of secret societies or in dissembling Democratic politicians.

IT IS STRIKING that among those who have expanded upon the two-party-system theory since its casual introduction by Potter over forty years ago, no one has laid emphasis on what had generally been touted as the key virtue of a two-party system, its control of extremism and its channeling of political conflict into moderate courses. Phillip Paludan did note that the "vital two-party system kept opposition within bounds by requiring platforms that spoke to the broad middle of the political spectrum, not to the extremes," and James McPherson mentioned their ability to "discipline" and "channel" political "activity."[28] There were good reasons for the other champions of the theory to avoid that obvious subject. Any case for moderation in Civil War political platforms would have to be made selectively. First, it has been notorious from 1864 to this day that the extremism of the Democratic platform in 1864 doomed that party to defeat in the presidential election. Second, for decades historians writing on the Civil War had depicted the history of the Republican party as a drama of confrontation between the radicals in the party and the president. So for much of the period of the war, radicalism within the Republican party had constituted a serious movement even if the radicals' inclinations to form a third-party ticket were finally stifled in September 1864. Third, by the time modern historians of the Civil War came to write about the virtues of the two-party system, in the 1960s and afterward, most of them were unembarrassed by what was defined as Republican "radicalism" in the Civil War era—championing equal rights for African Americans, for example—and therefore did not in this instance really see moderation as a virtue to be inculcated by party competition. Fourth, it was obvious, even when McKitrick first wrote on the subject a generation ago, that, as he expressed it, it "might even be said" of the radicals "that in the end they 'won.'"[29]

The first political historian to probe the weaknesses of the two-party-system theory, Michael F. Holt, explored the argument precisely at that vulnerable seam. In the end, he continued to endorse the thesis enthusiastically, but he felt that it offered no explanation of the lack of unity in the Republican party.[30] The logic of two-party competition also suggested that Republican policies should have grown more moderate rather than more radical. At bottom, the goad of party competition explains only the last-minute unification of the Republican or Union party in September 1864 for the presidential campaign and not the divisiveness within the party exemplified for two years up to that date.

IT IS IRONIC that McKitrick dwelt on accurate identification and on sure handling of the potentially disloyal opposition as one of the strengths of the two-party system; this celebrated feature even "had its lighter side," he said. Whatever the accomplishments of the system, accurate identification of disloyalty could not be numbered among them. In fact, a flailing inability to distinguish opposition from sedition was the aspect of political life in the North most threatening to unity and victory in the Civil War.

Treason was not a subject treated with lightheartedness in

the nineteenth century, either by those accused of it or by those making the accusation. And the misidentification of treason lay at the heart of the political problems between the parties in the North. Joseph Holt's apparently sincere misperception of opposition as sedition in the Old North-west, for example, made Salmon P. Chase believe civil war was only narrowly avoided in the North in 1864. Likewise, Democratic fears of Republican dynastic and despotic intentions caused them to invoke their right to bear arms and to bandy about some dangerously confrontational slogans in 1864: a fair election or a free fight, for example. Mistaken distrust of opposition as potential sedition or tyranny could lead to hair-trigger responses like those of Governor Yates, Governor Morton, or S. L. M. Barlow. Most important of all, mistaking organized political opposition for treason caused tens of thousands in the army in 1863 to threaten to march on their state legislatures if given the order.

Moderation simply was not a major part of the repertoire of nineteenth-century American political parties, and there was a steady continuity in style between the political slogans of counter-subversion in the 1850s and the political slogans of counter-subversion during the Civil War. The two-party system caused this. Carelessly pressing charges of treason and tyranny was the way the system worked at election time and had for years. That was politics as usual in the mid-nineteenth century.

American political parties in the Civil War era, it should be remembered, were in a stage of development not unlike the press or the capitalist economy itself of that day. They were as unregulated as the economy and as pre-modern as the press. Proponents of the two-party-system theory have failed to remind us adequately of the degree to which the nineteenth-century parties were unlike modern political parties.[31]

Here it is perhaps easiest to see the two-party-system theory sweeping historians off their feet. It can lead even to thoughtless acceptance of the patronage system before civil service reform.[32] We should not confuse that system for a program of management development or equal opportunity. Patronage did not cultivate future candidates for public office, and it did not study or attempt to improve government administration. No other part of the two-party system more merited the criticism that parties put self before commonwealth. That part of the system is best dismissed with derision, as political scientist Richard Franklin Bensel does, as a pre-modern and inefficient method of handling personnel.[33]

The operation of the New York Custom House reveals that the parties did not particularly infuse the organization with an ethic useful in winning wars; in fact, the placemen were not apparently infused with an ethic of patriotism or service at all. Leaders like Hiram Barney or Salmon P. Chase could be more idealistic than the humble party hacks behind the tariff duty desks, but the leaders were prone to using dangerous political tactics in electoral contests, as Simon Cameron's senate bid in 1863 showed vividly.

"Politics as usual" did not help the war effort conspicuously. Seeking patronage did not. Practicing brinksmanship did not. Shrieking treason did not. The ordinary working of the parties did not pose an insuperable impediment necessarily, either, but that is not the proposition on the table. The two-party-system theory is supposed to help explain northern victory, at a minimum, or even provide the "decisive" advantage. It does neither.

The obligatory rhetorical concessions to the legitimacy of the opposition, prevalent in modern party systems, were largely absent from party confrontations during the Civil War era. Their snarling and confrontational tone differed markedly from the decorous, humorous, and controlled tone of modern political debate. Nineteenth-century politicians did not often speak of their "worthy opponents" (except perhaps on the floor of Congress) or routinely profess respect for diversity of opinion on public issues. The modern discourse of pluralism and legitimacy did not yet exist. The modern avoidance of inflammatory and extremist language did not exist. And any strides made in that direction before the war were reversed during the war when many returned to the assumptions of the early republic that party opposition was illegitimate, factional, and potentially seditious. There was no noticeable difference in tone or practicality of dissent between the North with its two-party system and in the Confederacy without one. Wild but often heartfelt allegations of internal treason and tyrannical conspiracy were common on both sides of the Mason-Dixon Line.

Sadly, we must conclude that the major mysteries of Civil War politics remain unsolved. For the dominant two-party-system theory rested on the fundamental but unspoken assumption that political parties tended to moderate extremes, and it is the extremism of the Civil War political parties that to this day cries out for explanation. The power of the peace wing of the Democratic party was especially anomalous. That was the wing of the loyal opposition that so often verged on disloyalty, and there is simply no explaining the phenomenon to date. More even than the Republicans, who campaigned in 1864 as a Union party, the Democrats—as the "out's" attempting to get back "in" and fearful of losing competitiveness altogether—had every reason to contain their extremists for the sake of electability. And yet they could not agree on a moderate platform in 1864.

The Republicans, for their part, made mostly cosmetic gestures toward moderation and in fact rarely joined with the Douglas Democrats in a genuinely new mass coalition.[34] Instead, the stubborn resistance of the slave power drove the party into the arms of its radical antislavery wing, which held the plausible answers to the problem of victory over the Confederacy in emancipation, confiscation, and other "hard war" measures. Although it sometimes came dressed in the language of stern vindictiveness, Republican idealism, a greatly underestimated force in recent writing, triumphed in the Civil War.[35] That is not to say that politics was not fought hard and with the available tactics and tools. It is always important to remember of party "systems" that in terms of methods as opposed to ideology and platforms, both parties gave as good as they got during the nineteenth century.

IF THE TWO-PARTY system did not account for the beneficial effects of the political system on the northern war effort identified by McKitrick and others, what did? Three explanations merit further investigation.

First, emphasis on the parties has overshadowed the importance of the Constitution, both written and unwritten, in shaping the course of war and the northern victory. Second, the old theory mistakenly attributed to two-party competition what was really the fruit of one-party dominance. And, finally, we cannot underestimate the perverse role of stubborn Confederate resistance in hardening northern resolve.

The United States Constitution put the army and navy in the hands of a determined Republican commander-in-chief for four long years. That was the most important fact of political life in the Civil War. So important was it that its influence reached all the way to Richmond and silently shaped Confederate military strategy. It made a passive defense unacceptable in the South. No Confederate leader wanted to go to his people in the spring of 1861 with a plea to prepare for four solid years of bombardment and attack by northern arms and men. One or two years—or less if the United States had had a parliamentary system—might have been acceptable, but not four years. To avoid so bleak a prospect and bring the war to a more rapid close, the Confederacy would have to go on the tactical and strategic offensive.[36] Richmond did not explain the reason for this offensive strategy, in part because the Confederate leaders, too, had internalized the Constitution and knew without reflection or comment that Lincoln would be in office to oppose them for four years. In part also, Richmond did not explain because the leaders did not have to: they did not face an organized opposition party and their president enjoyed a six-year term and could not stand for reelection.

The significance of the four-year term for the northern commander-in-chief was not lost on British observers at the time, both hostile and sympathetic. This significance was easier to perceive from abroad because the British had a parliamentary rather than a presidential system. Even in the twentieth century, British commentators on the American Civil War were more likely to take note of the Union's fortunate constitutional circumstance. General Colin R. Ballard, among the first to recognize the "military genius" of Abraham Lincoln, was a British soldier who wrote not long after World War I. He pointed out in the beginning of his essay that in the United States "once elected the President holds the reins for four years; he can only be removed by impeachment; as he nominates and dismisses Ministers at his own will his power is almost unlimited . . . It is a matter of opinion whether a disguised autocracy is the best form of government in time of peace; history shows that in time of war it has many advantages."[37]

Such observations remind us as well of the importance of what the United States Constitution did not establish. The Constitution established a presidential rather than a parliamentary form of government for the United States. Confusion over this point dogged the two-party-system theory from the start, but the fact of the matter is that there was no serious alternative to the commander-in-chief in either the Confederacy or the Union, which on that point had identical constitutions. As for the North, surely most Americans would now agree that the lack of a parliamentary system with a ready alternative government waiting in the wings proved a godsend. Lincoln would otherwise likely have fallen from power after only six months in office, following Bull Run, and his government would certainly have failed after McClellan's defeat on the Peninsula at the end of June 1862. It is difficult to imagine what might have ensued, but it certainly is not easy to assume that the opposition party in the North would have brought about military victory quickly or emancipation at any time. The Constitution kept Lincoln in power even when his armies failed and his popularity waned, as both did repeatedly.

Like Great Britain, the United States also had an unwritten constitution. Political parties formed the most important part of the unwritten constitution of the United States by the time of the Civil War. More important for the outcome of the Civil War, however, was another part of the unwritten constitution, one of the major lessons politicians had learned from American party history up to that time: that failure to vote supplies for American troops in wartime was a recipe for political suicide. The death of the Federalist party after 1815 assured that for a century and a half the nominal power of Congress to control the army and navy by the power of the purse in fact proved not great enough to allow the legislative branch to shape wars in any significant way. Because the opposition party was helpless to influence the war through the Congress, it was left with nothing but impotent rage and debilitating factionalism, despite the customary unifying pressures that stemmed from being out of office. Those pressures were strong enough to make the party delay its nominating convention until the latest possible moment in the summer of 1864 to see which way the war was going. But when they were forced to act, the Democrats purchased unity at a price: by pitting a war candidate against his own peace platform, they suffered both public ridicule and historical disdain.

Next in importance to the role played by the United States Constitution, both written and unwritten, was the extent of political domination enjoyed by the Republican party throughout the nation in 1861. What was most notable about political power in the North after the secession of the southern states was the extent of one-party dominance. The strategic concentration of the Republican vote in the northern states had given Lincoln the electoral victory in 1860 despite gaining only 40 percent of the popular vote nationwide; with the departure of the Confederate States, that concentration was now puissant indeed. After the fall of Fort Sumter in 1861, Republicans held the governorships in 17 of the 19 states above the slaveholding border. If we exclude from the calculation the noncontiguous Pacific states, Republicans controlled *everything* but the border. They held the presidency, of course—that had precipitated southern secession in the first place—but because of the withdrawal of the southerners from Congress, the Republicans also held complete sway over both houses of the legislature. Democrats occupied fewer than 50 of 181 seats in the House of Representatives.[38] Only 14 Democrats were present in the Senate for the July 1861 special session of Congress.[39] Put simply and avoiding any counter-intuitive logic, Republican control smoothed the way for cooperation between Republican states and the Republican-controlled federal government for the war effort in the North.

Secure and overwhelming Republican control did have a down side for the war-making administration. It fostered struggles within the party that sometimes proved as threatening as criticism and opposition from the Democrats outside. Factionalism opened the door a little way to the Democrats in 1862, according to Lincoln, who cited as one of the three main reasons for Democratic resurgence in the off-year elections the criticism of the administration by its own press.[40] It posed a threat to continued Republican control again in the summer of 1864 with the formation of the radical third-party ticket of John C. Fremont and John Cochrane. And factionalism could threaten federal-state relations as well. Lincoln probably had more trouble dealing with Missouri than any other state that remained loyal to the Union, and there the Democratic party had been substantially removed from competition by a Unionist coup d'état in 1861 and continuing military pressure applied to put down guerrilla warfare. Yet no reader of Lincoln's extensive correspondence can come away from the more than 14,000 letters in the Library of Congress unimpressed by the disproportionate number from the different factions of Missouri's governing pro-Union party with their implacably troublesome demands.[41]

Finally, the radical direction in policy taken by the Republican party during the Civil War was less a product of Democratic opposition and competition than of Confederate resistance. McKitrick identified radicals as representing "the most articulate, most energetic, most militant wing of the Republican party," and their favorite policies, "emancipation, Negro troops, and confiscation of rebel property," were surely a help and not a hindrance to the Union war effort.[42] But, ironically, it was the Confederacy and not the dynamics of party competition that brought them to the fore. Most of these measures were resorted to only after Confederate resistance failed to be reduced by the government's initial measures. In other words, Confederate nationalism was far more powerful and more important than McKitrick deemed it, writing under the influence of the states'-rights internal-collapse theory of Frank Owsley. The radical policies of the Republicans in power during the war were also the products of Republican antislavery idealism—something never mentioned at all in McKitrick's explanation of Civil War politics and surely underestimated by the two-party-system theory.

THERE ARE MANY good reasons to celebrate the survival of the two-party system in the American Civil War, but we should avoid a careless presentism. The modernity of the institutions of Civil War America is easily exaggerated. We should always attempt to think of the era in a way that will make sense of Edwin M. Stanton's "Joshua letter" with its embrace of the old time religion and its scorn for "organizing victory." Even Republicans had their doubts about the staying power of capitalists in a long conflict, whatever their level of confidence in the ultimate advantages of industry and free labor in war. They did not think of themselves as organizers of victory, necessarily, but as courageous and virtuous fighters. Certainly the popular understanding of the war, as described in the press, was decidedly pre-modern and went surprisingly little beyond the ideals of chivalry.

Indeed, the pre-modern nature of the newspapers of the era explains much that is otherwise anomalous in the Civil War. It explains the pre-modern view of press freedom that dominated Republican understanding and put the era closer to the early republic with its doctrines of seditious libel. And what kept the press in pre-modernity was the political parties to which it was enthralled.

As for the political parties themselves, in actual structure and function as well as in terms of popular understanding they fell somewhere between the "system" as understood by modern social science and the deleterious factions that dominated the political imaginations of the early republic. Thus, the celebrated two-party-system in fact did nothing to guarantee its own survival. At first, politicians thought it best perhaps to put the parties "on hold" until war's end, but that resolve foundered when the war's end proved distant instead of near, when elections loomed with their accustomed lures of power and office, and when party operatives and the American people, who had internalized the Constitution's inexorable election clock, insisted on political business as usual. When politics then performed as usual, ironically, many were shocked, hoped for the effective end of opposition, and even threatened to eliminate it if it proved obstructionist.

Some politicians thereafter thought only of electoral victory in the short term and not of the long-run survival of a superior political system guided by two-party political competition. The party system itself made no marked contribution to Union victory, and at a few dangerous moments its accustomed operation threatened political suicide.

NOTES

Introduction

1 Roy P. Basler, ed., *The Collected Works of Abraham Lincoln,* 9 vols. (New Brunswick, New Jersey: Rutgers University Press, 1953–55), VIII, 100.

2 George E. Baker, ed., *The Works of William H. Seward,* 5 vols. (Boston: Houghton, Mifflin, 1883–1884), V, 493.

3 Ibid., 496–497.

4 Ibid., 500.

5 Michael F. Holt, "Abraham Lincoln and the Politics of Union," in John L. Thomas, ed., *Abraham Lincoln and the American Political Tradition* (Amherst, Massachusetts: University of Massachusetts Press, 1986), p. 111.

6 Phillip Shaw Paludan, *"A People's Contest": The Union and Civil War, 1861–1865* (New York: Harper & Row, 1988), p. 78.

7 Basler, ed., *Coll. Works of Abraham Lincoln,* VIII, 100.

8 Italics mine. For more description of their views, see Chapter 7 of this book.

9 Michael F. Holt, "An Elusive Synthesis: Northern Politics during the Civil War," in James M. McPherson and William J. Cooper, Jr., eds., *Writing the Civil War: The Quest to Understand* (Columbia, South Carolina: University of South Carolina Press, 1998), p. 112.

10 George C. Rable, *The Confederate Republic: A Revolution against Politics* (Chapel Hill: University of North Carolina Press, 1994), esp. pp. 210–212.

11 Richard Franklin Bensel, *Yankee Leviathan: The Origins of Central State Authority in America, 1859-1877* (New York: Cambridge University Press, 1990), pp. 228–233.

1 "No party now but all for our country"

1 Michael F. Holt calls for injecting more of "a perception of political flux and uncertainty during the war years." "Neither northern voters nor politicians living during the Civil War," he says, " . . . could be sure that either the voter alignments of 1860 *or the existing political parties* . . . would endure. An appreciation and exploitation of that uncertainty . . . offers the best chance of synthesizing the diverse literature written by 'new political historians' and by fans of the realignment/party system paradigm." Holt, "An Elusive Synthesis: Northern Politics during the Civil War," in James M. McPherson and William J. Cooper, Jr., eds., *Writing the Civil War: The Quest to Understand* (Columbia, South Carolina: University of South Carolina Press, 1998), p. 126. See also Glenn C. Altschuler and Stuart M. Blumin, *Rude Republic: Americans and Their Politics in the Nineteenth Century* (Princeton, NJ: Princeton University Press, 2000), pp. 10, 47, 169.

2 Chicago *Tribune,* April 15 and 16, 1861.

3 Jacob E. Cooke, ed., *The Federalist* (Middletown, Connecticut: Wesleyan University Press, 1961), p. 346.

4 Francis Lieber, *Manual of Political Ethics,* 2 vols. (Boston: Charles C. Little and James Brown, 1838–1839), II, 414, 415.

5 Ibid., 444–445.

6 Arthur M. Schlesinger, Jr., and Fred L. Israel, eds., *History of American Presidential Elections, 1789–1968,* 4 vols. (New York: Chelsea House, 1971), II, 1183.

7 I treated the subject more fully in "The Civil War and the Two-Party System," in James M. McPherson, ed., *"We Cannot*

Escape History": Lincoln and the Last Best Hope of Earth (Urbana: University of Illinois Press, 1995), pp. 90–91.

8 Roy P. Basler, ed., *The Collected Works of Abraham Lincoln,* 9 vols. (New Brunswick, New Jersey: Rutgers University Press, 1953–1955), II, 126.

9 New York *Times,* August 14, 1861.

10 Michael Burlingame, ed., *Lincoln's Journalist: John Hay's Anonymous Writings for the Press, 1860–1864* (Carbondale, Illinois: Southern Illinois University Press, 1998), pp. 196–197.

11 Phillip Shaw Paludan, *"A People's Contest": The Union and Civil War, 1861–1865* (New York: Harper & Row, 1988), p. 85. The lengthiest treatment of anti-party sentiment in the war appears in Joel H. Silbey, *A Respectable Minority: The Democratic Party in the Civil War Era, 1860–1868* (New York: W. W. Norton, 1977), pp. 39–49. Silbey regarded such sentiments as mostly a "Republican tactic" (p. 42) that was essentially dead by "the middle of 1862" when "the imperatives of the political culture and structure were at work" (p. 61). Later, in *The American Political Nation, 1838–1893* (Stanford, California: Stanford University Press, 1991), p. 42, Silbey stressed "the American acceptance of party" after 1840: "There was no receding, or let up, thereafter. By the middle 1840's, the case for party was prominent and routine, [and] the intellectual underpinnings were clear." Silbey made no exception of the Civil War period (pp. 9, 139). Paludan insisted that "by the mid-nineteenth century Americans had developed wide-spread devotion to the political culture of the nation. Reformers might attack the party system as insensitive to moral values, and Republicans especially had their share of antiparty rhetoric. But for the most part Northerners extolled their party system" (p. 14).

12 *Wilkes' Spirit of the Times,* April 27, 1861.

13 Chicago *Tribune,* August 9 and 25, 1861.

14 On Pittsburgh politics and the no-party ideal I follow leads provided in a seminar paper by Ted Timmerman, "There Is No Doubt Great Horror in Civil War, but Bad Domestic Boils

Are Very Hard to Stomach," History 597, Penn State University, spring 2001.

15 Pittsburgh *Gazette,* October 1 and 4, 1861.

16 York *Gazette,* June 18 and 25, 1861. Contrast with the Pittsburgh *Post,* esp. August 27, 1861. "It means . . . no party but the Republican party," said York's Democrats.

17 Pittsburgh *Gazette,* October 2, 1861.

18 Pittsburgh *Post,* June 18, 1862.

19 New York *World,* May 8, 1862. On the *World's* ownership and editorial party commitment see George T. McJimsey, *Genteel Partisan: Manton Marble, 1834–1917* (Ames: Iowa State University Press, 1971), pp. 24–41.

20 New York *World,* June 30, 1862.

21 New York *Times,* July 1 and 2, 1862.

22 See, for example, New York *World,* September 10, 11, 12, 15, and 16; October 7, 1862.

23 Edward Everett to George S. Hillard, September 10, 1861, Papers of Edward Everett, Massachusetts Historical Society, microfilm reel 18. Everett was willing to have the letter read aloud to the meeting but did not want it published. In oratory of about the same time he sometimes spoke as though party opposition was inevitable. See Edward Everett, *The Great Issues Now before the Country: An Oration . . . Delivered at the New York Academy of Music. July 4, 1861* (New York: James G. Gregory, 1861), p. 4. In other versions, the speech was called *The Questions of the Day.*

24 C. A. Reed to Lyman Trumbull, June 17, 1862, Lyman Trumbull Papers, Library of Congress, microfilm reel 13.

25 Silbey, *A Respectable Minority,* pp. 55–59, describes the no-party position of the War Democrats from the Democratic point of view.

26 New York *Evening Post,* September 11, 1862; the article was quoted favorably in the Democratic *World.*

27 New York *Evening Post,* September 29, 1862.

28 New York *Times,* October 14, 1862.

29 On the propensity to "ride a hobby" see J. Mills Thornton, III, *Politics and Power in a Slave Society: Alabama, 1800–1860* (Baton Rouge: Louisiana State University Press, 1978), p. 71.

30 See Reinhard H. Luthin and Harry J. Carman, *Lincoln and the Patronage* (New York: Columbia University Press, 1943), and Paul P. Van Riper and Harry N. Scheiber, "The Confederate Civil Service," *Journal of Southern History,* 25 (November 1959), 448–470.

31 On Democratic corruption in the Buchanan administration see Mark W. Summers, *The Plundering Generation: Corruption and the Crisis of the Union, 1849–1861* (New York: Oxford University Press, 1987), and Michael F. Holt, *The Political Crisis of the 1850s* (New York: W. W. Norton, 1978), p. 215.

32 Carman and Luthin in *Lincoln and the Patronage,* p. 330, termed it "an almost complete sweep if allowance is made for the vacancies in the South occasioned by the Secession." Holt, despite an interest in "Abraham Lincoln and the Politics of Union," p. 127, in finding initiative from Lincoln in reaching out to Democrats to form a Union party on grounds different from the anti-southern Republican party he inherited, repeated the common wisdom: "It is true that outside of the border states the vast majority of civilian positions went to regular Republicans recommended by Republican congressmen."

33 Fish stated that "when it is remembered that to many posts in the South no appointments could be made, and that consequently no removals are noted, it will be seen that the sweep was the most thoroughgoing that had ever been made; indeed, it was almost complete." *The Civil Service and the Patronage* (Cambridge: Harvard University Press, 1920), p. 170. Fish had earlier described the "pressure for a 'clean sweep'" as "insistent." "Lincoln and the Patronage," *American Historical Review,* 8 (October 1902), 54, 57.

34 Carl Russell Fish, "Table of Removals," *Annual Report of the American Historical Association,* I (1899), 82. See also Fish, "Lin-

coln and the Patronage," 53–69, and *The Civil Service and the Patronage* (Cambridge: Harvard University Press, 1920), esp. p. 170.

35 Luthin and Carman, *Lincoln and the Patronage,* p. 60.

36 *Register of Officers and Agents, Civil, Military, and Naval, in the Service of the United States on the Thirtieth of September, 1861* (Washington, D.C.: Government Printing Office, 1862). The work that follows in this chapter is based on this and other years' volumes. Cited as *Official Register* hereafter.

37 All federal employees are listed. They are not identified by party affiliation; I have assumed that the incumbents after so many years of Democratic control were all Democrats. The new Republican regime did not report that there were any Republicans present in the custom house when they took over operation.

38 David Wilmot to Hiram Barney, May 1, 1861, Hiram Barney Papers, box 30, Huntington Library, San Marino, California.

39 Resolutions of a public meeting of Republicans of the Eighth Ward, Brooklyn, Hiram Barney Papers, box 12. The motion to reconsider the censure passed 45–11.

40 "One Who Knows" to Hiram Barney, 1861, Hiram Barney Papers, box 33.

41 A. Gregory et al. to Hiram Barney, June 27, 1861, Hiram Barney Papers, box 33.

42 Thomas Van Buren to Hiram Barney, May 8, 1861, Hiram Barney Papers, box 33.

43 S. C. Johnson to Hiram Barney, May 16, 1861, Hiram Barney Papers, box 33.

44 Amasa J. Parker to Hiram Barney, September 30, 1861, Hiram Barney Papers, box 24.

45 R. McCormick to A. M. Palmer, November 18, 1862, Hiram Barney Papers, box 33.

46 J. A. Kennedy to Hiram Barney, May 25, 1861, Hiram Barney Papers, box 33.

47 R. McCormick to A. M. Palmer, November 18, 1862, Hiram
   Barney Papers, box 33.

48 James Kelly to William H. Seward, August 12, 1864, Abraham
   Lincoln Papers, Library of Congress, microfilm reel 79.

49 John A. Gray to Montgomery Blair, August 20, 1864, Abraham
   Lincoln Papers, microfilm reel 79.

50 Hiram Barney to Edward C. Delavan, February 17, 1864,
   Hiram Barney Papers, box 2. For an account of Barney's removal that fails to realize that the ideal of nonpartisanship
   was construed as lack of leadership see Carman and Luthin,
   Lincoln and the Patronage, pp. 278–280.

51 Percentages based on a study of the *Official Register.*

52 See Salmon P. Chase to ?, September 22, 1862, Salmon P.
   Chase Papers, John Niven, ed., microfilm reel 23, refusing to
   interfere in the collector's patronage. But compare with his
   letter on California patronage (Chase to Samuel L. Bridge,
   July 10, 1862, Chase Papers, reel 21) insisting that "in the present circumstances of the country there is no choice politically, in my judgment, except between the Republican Party,
   and the so-called Democratic Party," and informing Bridge, "I
   could not select you for a political position . . . if indeed you
   favor the Democratic Party as now constituted."

53 I am indebted to J. Mills Thornton's analysis of political parties in Alabama for the different ideals of party workers and
   candidates, definitely favoring the vision of the candidates,
   that underlies this analysis of the working of the custom
   house. See *Politics and Power in a Slave Society: Alabama, 1800–
   1860* (Baton Rouge: Louisiana State University Press, 1978),
   esp. pp. 131–132. On the "party imperative," see Joel H. Silbey,
   The American Political Nation, 1838–1893 (Stanford: Stanford
   University Press, 1991), p. 139.

54 Hiram Barney to Abraham Lincoln, January 9, 1864, Abraham
   Lincoln Papers, microfilm reel 65.

55 New York *Evening Post,* May 27, 1863.

56 John Lorimer Graham to Hiram Barney, March 31, 1862, Hiram Barney Papers, box 18.

57 William Cullen Bryant to Hiram Barney, May 28, 1863, Hiram Barney Papers, box 1.

58 Amasa J. Parker to Hiram Barney, September 30, 1861, Hiram Barney Papers, box 24.

59 Again, I am indebted to J. Mills Thornton's analysis of party. Chester Arthur, as historian Mike Smith reminded me, was a later exception.

60 Frank W. Ballard to Hiram Barney, March 11, 1861, Hiram Barney Papers, box 13.

61 Luke Gore to Hiram Barney, August 3, 1862, Hiram Barney Papers, box 33. The reference is not clear and may have referred to a state draft.

62 Ambrose H. Cole to Hiram Barney, August 5, 1862, Hiram Barney Papers, box 15.

63 Edward B. Northrup to Hiram Barney, November 17, 1862, Hiram Barney Papers, box 33.

64 D. M. Nagle to Hiram Barney, April 2, 1862, Hiram Barney Papers, box 33.

65 T. Bailey Myers to Hiram Barney, December 11, 1861, Hiram Barney Papers, box 33.

66 Louis Ruttkay to Hiram Barney, November 21, 1864, Hiram Barney Papers, box 33.

67 To be sure, state governments in the Confederacy declared an unconscionable number of state workers essential and exempt from Confederate conscription.

68 Basler, ed., *Coll. Works of Abraham Lincoln,* VI, 346.

69 The civil service historian Carl Russell Fish condemned Lincoln for deciding to consider military service in making appointments, saying, "This claim, widely acknowledged, has caused incalculable harm to public service, and yet seems so reasonable and proper that reformers have many times been obliged to comply with it." "Lincoln and the Patronage," 68.

70 New York *Evening Post,* July 13, 1863.

71 Robert H. T. Liepold to Abraham Lincoln, February 27, 1864, and October 7, 1864, Abraham Lincoln Papers, microfilm reels 69 and 83, respectively.

72 This confirms the view of Mark W. Summers, who alleges that corrupt practices "were abuses inseparable from the whole principle that office was a reward rather than a sacred trust, a political plum rather than a public service." *The Plundering Generation: Corruption and the Crisis of the Union, 1849–1861* (New York: Oxford University Press, 1987), p. 29.

73 What follows is based on "Custom House Frauds. Investigation by E. Jordan, Solicitor of the Treasury," 130-page ms report, ca. Dec. 1862–Jan. 1863, Hiram Barney Papers, box 32.

74 For an example of carrying the two-party-system thesis so far as to appear to glorify the patronage system, see Paludan, *"A People's Contest,"* p. 378: "It also opened career and patronage to those ambitious men who played by the rules."

2 *"Blustering treason in every assembly"*

1 James G. Randall, *Constitutional Problems under Lincoln* (1951; Urbana: University of Illinois Press, 1964); Arthur Bestor, "The American Civil War as a Constitutional Crisis," *American Historical Review,* 69 (January 1964), 327–352; Harold M. Hyman, *A More Perfect Union: The Impact of the Civil War and Reconstruction on the Constitution* (New York: Alfred A. Knopf, 1973), esp p. xvii. Other works could well be cited, but these provide the shape of the historical debate.

2 Michael Kammen, *A Machine That Would Go of Itself: The Constitution in American Culture* (New York: Alfred A. Knopf, 1986), p. 3 and *passim,* argued that public opinion in America has generally expressed reverence for the Constitution while knowing little about it.

3 Roy Franklin Nichols, *The Disruption of American Democracy* (New York: Free Press, 1948), pp. 20–22.

4 Ibid., p. 20. A preliminary application of Nichols's insight into the Civil War appeared in my article "The Civil War and

the Two-Party System," in James M. McPherson, ed., *"We Cannot Escape History": Lincoln and the Last Best Hope of Earth* (Urbana: University of Illinois Press, 1995), p. 92.

5 Article II, section 1, of the Constitution requires the presidential election to be held on the same day "throughout the United States," but that refers to the count in the electoral college and not to the selection of the presidential electors. That was left to the states and not standardized until 1848.

6 New York *Evening Post,* July 21, 1862.

7 Lyman Trumbull to Abraham Lincoln, September 7, 1862, Abraham Lincoln Papers, Library of Congress, microfilm reel 41.

8 Allan Nevins, *The War for the Union: Volume II, War Becomes Revolution* (New York: Charles Scribner's Sons, 1960), pp. 390–392.

9 "Patriotic Resolutions of the Officers & Men of Illinois Regiments Corinth, Miss.," January 30, 1863, Abraham Lincoln Papers, microfilm reel 48. Since my initial treatment of the soldiers' resolutions I encountered in the Abraham Lincoln Papers, discussed in my article "The Civil war and the Two-Party System," pp. 96–97, I have uncovered dozens more in other sources, and I therefore expand on my earlier introduction to the subject here.

10 *Resolutions on the Conduct of the War, Adopted by the Officers and Enlisted Men from Illinois, stationed at Bolivar, Tennessee,* February 13, 1863, Abraham Lincoln Papers, microfilm reel 48.

11 "Resolutions of the 82nd Illinois regiment," February 14, 1863, Lyman Trumbull Papers, microfilm reel 14.

12 Chicago *Tribune,* April 1, 1863.

13 Ibid., March 25, 1863.

14 Ibid., April 22, 1863.

15 The infantry regiments were the following: 7, 8, 9, 12, 13, 14, 15, 16, 17, 18, 20, 22, 27, 32, 36, 38, 39, 41, 42 (officers only), 43, 46, 47, 50, 51, 52, 54, 55, 56, 57, 61, 62 (officers and one company of men only), 64, 66, 72, 73, 76, 82, 84, 88, 92, 95, 96, 103, 107, 108, 111, 113, 115, 116, 117, 119, 124, 126, 127, 130. Artillery included: Co.

A, Chicago Light Artillery; Co. B, Illinois Light Artillery; Co. H, 1 Illinois Battery; Vaughan's Battery. Cavalry included: 6, 8, 11, and Merrill's Horse. The resolutions were usually reported in the Chicago *Tribune.*

16 I am indebted to Earl J. Hess, *The Union Soldier in Battle: Enduring the Ordeal of Combat* (Lawrence: University Press of Kansas, 1997), esp. p. 64, for making clear the phenomenon of winter quarters.

17 Horace Porter, *Campaigning with Grant* (1897; Lincoln: University of Nebraska Press, 2000), pp. 329–330.

18 James M. McPherson, *What They Fought For, 1861–1865* (Baton Rouge: Louisiana State University Press, 1994), p. 4.

19 I discussed the process of adoption of the resolutions within the regiments in "The Civil War and the Two-Party System," in James M. McPherson, ed., *"We Cannot Escape History": Lincoln and the Last Best Hope of Earth* (Urbana: University of Illinois Press, 1995), pp. 86–104.

20 Indiana regiments were also affected, though less dramatically than those from Illinois. I found resolutions from five infantry regiments (14, 33, 50, 58, and 84). Four Ohio infantry regiments sent resolutions (17, 31, 38, 71) along with three batteries (7, 9, 14). Three Iowa infantry regiments (2, 27, and 39) as well as the 3rd Michigan Cavalry and the 7th Wisconsin Battery sent resolutions. In addition, the 100th, 149th, 150th, and 176th Pennsylvania Infantry regiments, the 11th New Jersey, the 7th and 12th Connecticut (officers only), and the 2nd Regiment of the New York State Militia sent resolutions reassuring the people of their loyalty and approving government policies (generally less threatening in tone). They were reported in the New York *Tribune* of March 25, 1863. Altogether 88 units were represented (counting the Illinois units listed in an earlier note).

21 Glenn C. Altschuler and Stuart M. Blumin, *Rude Republic: Americans and Their Politics in the Nineteenth Century* (Princeton: Princeton University Press, 2000), p. 4.

22 York (Pennsylvania) *Gazette,* March 10, 1863; April 14, 1863; and June 16, 1863.

23 New York *World,* March 9, 1863.

24 First published by Crissey & Markley in Philadelphia, *No Party Now but All for Our Country* was reprinted in a revised edition in New York in May by the Loyal Publication Society, of which Lieber was a board member (printed by Westcott & Company). I examined Lieber's retained copies at the Huntington Library, San Marino, California. It is reprinted as "probably the most widely circulated speech of the 1864 campaign" in Arthur M. Schlesinger, Jr., and Fred L. Israel, eds., *History of American Presidential Elections, 1789–1968,* 4 vols. (New York: Chelsea House, 1971), II, 1181–1189.

25 New York *Evening Post,* May 16, 1863. Bellows went on to say that the initial fear had lapsed—thinking of the defeat of the Peace Democrat Thomas Seymour in the Connecticut gubernatorial election that spring.

26 New York *World,* November 21, 1864.

27 Erwin Stanley Bradley, *Simon Cameron, Lincoln's Secretary of War: A Political Biography* (Philadelphia: University of Pennsylvania Press, 1966), pp. 42–49.

28 Bradley, *Simon Cameron,* pp. 115–121.

29 S. H. Fink to Simon Cameron, October 29, 1862, Correspondence and Papers of Simon Cameron, Historical Society of Dauphin County, Harrisburg, Pennsylvania, microfilm edition by Pennsylvania Historical and Museum Commission, reel 8. Hereafter cited as Simon Cameron Papers.

30 D. G. Walton to Simon Cameron, November 18, 1862, Simon Cameron Papers, microfilm reel 8.

31 Benjamin H. Brewster to Simon Cameron, January 14, 1863, Simon Cameron Papers, microfilm reel 8.

32 W. M. Wiley to Simon Cameron, December 7, 1862, Simon Cameron Papers, microfilm reel 8.

33 Samuel Young to Simon Cameron, November 18, 1862, Simon Cameron Papers, microfilm reel 8.

34 Bradley, *Simon Cameron,* pp. 225–232.

35 S. C. Purviance to J. D. Cameron, November 1, 1862, Simon Cameron Papers, microfilm reel 8.

36 George W. Weaver to Simon Cameron, November 29, 1862, Simon Cameron Papers, microfilm reel 8.

37 S. John to Simon Cameron, January 15, 1863, Simon Cameron Papers, microfilm reel 8.

38 William T. Herfenton to Simon Cameron, January 17, 1863, Simon Cameron Papers, microfilm reel 8.

39 Bradley, *Simon Cameron,* p. 230.

40 Oliver P. Morton to Edwin M. Stanton, June 25, 1862, and to Abraham Lincoln, June 25, 1862, Abraham Lincoln Papers, microfilm reel 37.

41 See Richard Yates to Abraham Lincoln, January 30, 1863; William Butler, Ozias M. Hatch, and Jesse K. Dubois to Abraham Lincoln, March 1, 1863 (with Yates endorsement), Abraham Lincoln Papers, microfilm reel 49.

42 Richard Yates to Edwin M. Stanton, August 17, 1863, *Official Records,* III, 3, p. 685.

43 Michael F. Holt, "Making and Mobilizing the Republican Party, 1854–1860," in Robert F. Engs and Randall M. Miller, eds., *The Genesis of Republicanism: The Birth and Growth of the Grand Old Party, 1854–1872* (Philadelphia: University of Pennsylvania Press, 2002). See William Gienapp, *The Origins of the Republican Party, 1852–1856* (New York: Oxford University Press, 1987), pp. 92–100.

44 Gienapp, *The Origins of the Republican Party, 1852–1856,* pp. 295–303.

45 See Chapter 7, note 22.

46 Eric L. McKitrick, "Party Politics and the Union and Confederate War Efforts," in William Nisbet Chambers and Walter Dean Burnham, eds., *The American Party Systems: Stages of Political Development* (New York: Oxford University Press, 1967), p. 141.

47 Such was the conclusion of the scholar who studied the sub-

ject most closely, Frank Klement. See works by him in Chapter 5, note 3.

3 "He must be entrenching"

1 Indeed, recent theories of nationalism—and the Civil War was a landmark of American nationalism—emphasize the role of public communications in its creation. See Anthony D. Smith, *Nationalism and Modernism: A Critical Survey of Recent Theories of Nations and Nationalism* (London: Routledge, 1998), p. 33, and Ernest Gellner, "Nationalism and Modernization," in John Hutchinson and Anthony D. Smith, eds., *Nationalism* (Oxford: Oxford University Press, 1994), pp. 54-63.

2 James M. Perry, *A Bohemian Brigade: The Civil War Correspondents—Mostly Rough, Sometimes Ready* (New York: John Wiley & Sons, 2000), p. x. Allan Nevins noted that "One of the greatest indirect contributions to the war strength of the nation was made by the press . . . It kept the people informed, it more than any other agency molded public sentiment, and despite shrill dissident voices and conflicting policies, it crystallized a spirit of national unity." *The War for the Union: Volume I, The Improvised War, 1861–1862* (New York: Charles Scribner's Sons, 1959), p. 261. He noted its contributions to "unity" without explaining how a sharply divided partisan press brought such unity about.

3 See especially Michael Schudson, *The Good Citizen: A History of American Civic Life* (New York: Free Press, 1998), pp. 120-126, where he points out that the "political independence of which penny papers boasted was the wave of the future in newspaper publishing, but it would be a long time coming. Newspaper editors preached independence but practiced partisanship." By combining a study of civic culture with the history of journalism, Schudson has brought together the most balanced depiction of journalism available. His view is considerably altered from his earlier book, *Discovering the News: A So-*

cial History of American Newspapers (New York: Basic Books, 1978).

4 Schudson, *The Good Citizen,* p. 121.

5 Lambert A. Wilmer, *Our Press Gang: Or a Complete Exposition of the Corruptions and Crimes of the American Newspapers* (Philadelphia: J. T. Lloyd, 1859), p. 209.

6 For a case study of the inability of a newspaper to make headway in New York in the Civil War period without succumbing to party connection, see George T. McJimsey, *Genteel Partisan: Manton Marble, 1834–1917* (Ames: Iowa State University Press, 1971), pp. 37–39.

7 Brayton Harris, *Blue & Gray in Black and White: Newspapers in the Civil War* (Washington, D.C.: Batsford Brassey, 1999), p. 15.

8 For this image of the press see in addition to Schudson's excellent book, J. Cutler Andrews's pioneering *The North Reports the Civil War* (Pittsburgh: University of Pittsburgh Press, 1955), and *The South Reports the Civil War* (1970; Pittsburgh: University of Pittsburgh Press, 1985).

9 Wilmer, *Our Press Gang,* p. 200.

10 Harrisburg *Telegraph,* June 24, 1864.

11 William Howard Russell, *My Diary North and South* (Boston: T.O.H.P. Burnham, 1863), p. 435.

12 George Wilkes, *The Great Battle Fought at Manassas . . . July 21st, 1861* (New York: Brown & Ryan, 1861), and Edmund Clarence Stedman, *The Battle of Bull Run* (New York: Rudd & Carleton, 1861). On Wilkes see Patricia Cline Cohen, *The Murder of Helen Jewett: The Life and Death of a Prostitute in Nineteenth-Century New York* (New York: Random House, 1998), pp. 128, 203–204, 218. On Stedman see Dumas Malone, ed., *Dictionary of American Biography,* 20 vols. (New York: Charles Scribner's Sons, 1935), XVII, 552–553.

13 James M. Perry, *A Bohemian Brigade: The Civil War Correspondents—Mostly Rough, Sometimes Ready* (New York: John Wiley & Sons, 2000), p. 33.

14 I am deeply indebted to a brilliant new literature that blends
military, political, and cultural analysis of the war and under-
mines the conventional interpretation of northern victory as
a progress from the conservative tactics of George B.
McClellan on the Peninsula to the radically destructive tactics
of Ulysses S. Grant and William T. Sherman. Modern cultural
analysis of the war began with Michael C. C. Adams's *Our
Masters the Rebels: A Speculation on Union Military Failure in the
East, 1861–1865* (Cambridge: Harvard University Press, 1978),
now retitled *Fighting for Defeat.* Bruce Tap in *Over Lincoln's
Shoulder: The Committee on the Conduct of the War* (Lawrence:
University Press of Kansas, 1998), pp. 124, 137, criticized the
Joint Committee on the Conduct of the War for reinforcing
"amateurish and naive opinions about warfare" and failing
"to comprehend that aggressiveness without a proper understanding of the realities of strategy and weaponry could be a
detriment to northern forces." Eric T. Dean in "'We Live under a Government of Men and Morning Newspapers': Image,
Expectation, and the Peninsula Campaign of 1862," *Virginia
Magazine of History and Biography,* 103 (January 1995), 14,
identified the penny press as the culprit for leading to a preference for "hard fighting" and "a general denigration of strategy and delay," along with associating West Point-educated
generals with "procrastination." Also suggestive is Chapter 7
on the "Sword and Shovel" in Gerald Linderman's influential
*Embattled Courage: The Experience of Combat in the American Civil
War* (New York: Free Press, 1987).

15 New York *Times,* August 21, 1861.

16 See for example New York *Tribune,* July 25, 1861; New York *Evening Post,* July 25, 1861; New York *Times,* July 26 and 29, 1861.

17 These psychological lessons are essentially the opposites of
the defeatism and fear of the Confederates identified by Michael C. C. Adams in *Our Masters the Rebels,* but I was first
stimulated to examine the question by his brilliant discoveries about the cultural expectations of the North in the war.

18 New York *Times,* July 29, 1861.

19 New York *Evening Post,* July 24, 1861.

20 Ibid., July 23, 1861.

21 New York *Tribune,* July 23, 1861. For complaints that the Confederates hid behind entrenchments, see July 29 and August 2.

22 Despite what he told the press, General McClellan in fact attempted to decrease the ratio of rifled cannons to smoothbores, without success. On such dysfunctional technology in weaponry see Paddy Griffith, *Battle Tactics of the Civil War* (1987; New Haven: Yale University Press, 1989), p. 169. Linderman's *Embattled Courage* brilliantly called the attention of historians to the ethic of courage internalized by soldiers in the war, but I want here to explore its origins in the humiliation of Bull Run cowardice and also its development over time in the popular imagination.

23 "The Advantages of Defeat," *Atlantic Monthly,* 8 (September 1861), 364. George M. Fredrickson in *The Inner Civil War: Northern Intellectuals and the Crisis of the Union* (New York: Harper & Row, 1965), pp. 74-75, made historians aware of this important article but misinterpreted it, finding only authoritarianism and Darwinism where there was also antislavery zeal and romanticism. On Norton see the unadmiring sketch on pp. 31-32 of Fredrickson's book.

24 *Wilkes' Spirit of the Times,* April 27, 1861.

25 Ibid.

26 New York *Evening Post,* May 17, 1862. The paper clung to the wisdom: "The test of merit with the private soldier is held to be in the use of the bayonet: it is undeniable that in this war the rebel soldiers . . . have fled before the bayonets of our men." New York *Evening Post,* October 18, 1862.

27 On the language see Paul Fussell, *The Great War and Modern Memory* (London: Oxford University Press, 1975), pp. 21-22.

28 John Keegan, *The Mask of Command* (New York: Viking, 1987), p. 169.

29 Chicago *Tribune,* August 8, 1861.

30 George Wilkes, *McClellan: From Ball's Bluff to Antietam* (New York: Sinclair Tousey, 1863), p. 3.

31 Ibid., p. 10.

32 Wilkes, *McClellan*, pp. 13, 14, 16. See also p. 8.

33 Ibid., pp. 13, 15.

34 Ibid., p. 37.

35 Van Buren Denslow, *Fremont and McClellan: Their Political and Military Careers Reviewed*, 2nd ed. (Yonkers, New York: Office of the *Clarion*, 1862). The material had first been published in the newspaper, and the resulting 32-page pamphlet sold for ten cents.

36 Wilkes spoke of "strategic generals" as conservatives once in *McClellan*, p. 33.

37 Denslow, *Fremont and McClellan*, pp. 13, 19, 24.

38 Ibid., p. 10.

39 Bernard F. Reilly, Jr., *Political Prints, 1766–1876: Catalog of the Collections in the Library of Congress* (Boston: G. K. Hall, 1991), p. 490.

40 Tap, *Over Lincoln's Shoulder*, p. 124.

41 The speech was reprinted in the New York *Tribune* and *Herald*, and considered so telling after that, that the *Evening Post* also reprinted most of it on August 6 (from which version the quotations here are taken).

42 *Congressional Globe,* 37 Cong., 3 sess., pp. 3386–3392.

43 Zachariah Chandler to Abraham Lincoln, August 8, 1862, Abraham Lincoln Papers, microfilm reel 39.

44 Both Bruce Tap and Eric T. Dean note this theme of prejudice against West Point.

45 *Cong. Globe,* 37 Cong., 3 sess., p. 324.

46 Ibid., p. 330.

47 Abraham Lincoln to Carl Schurz, November 12, 1862, in Basler, ed., *Coll. Works of Abraham Lincoln,* V, 494.

48 See, for example, John F. Reynolds, "Consolidated Morning Report of First Army Corps near Sharpsburg, October 1, 1862," Abraham Lincoln Papers, microfilm reel 42. See also

Reynolds to Lorenzo Williams, October 3, 1862, and other "Field Returns" at October 3, 1862, in the same collection.

49 Basler, ed., *Coll. Works of Abraham Lincoln*, V, 484.

50 Don E. Fehrenbacher and Virginia Fehrenbacher, eds., *Recollected Words of Abraham Lincoln* (Stanford: Stanford University Press, 1996), pp. 300–301.

51 Theodore Calvin Pease and James G. Randall, eds., *The Diary of Orville Hickman Browning*, 2 vols. (Springfield: Illinois State Historical Library, 1925–1933), I, 595–595.

52 Students of the election of 1864 usually focus on the Republicans' attempt to depict the Democratic party as disloyal and have thus underestimated the importance of the devastating critique of McClellan's military reputation. William Frank Zornow created the classic interpretation of Republican political strategy in *Lincoln and the Party Divided* (Norman: University of Oklahoma Press, 1954).

53 William Swinton, *McClellan's Military Career Reviewed and Exposed* (Washington: Union Congressional Committee, 1864).

54 Ibid., pp. 18, 19, 20.

55 [James Russell Lowell], "General McClellan's Report," *North American Review*, 98 (April 1864), 564.

56 Arthur M. Schlesinger, Jr., and Fred L. Israel, eds., *History of American Presidential Elections, 1789–1968*, 4 vols. (New York: Chelsea House, 1971), II, 1201, 1202.

57 Until the work of Bruce Tap, the party origins of this military critique remained substantially overlooked. Joseph L. Harsh, "On the McClellan-Go-Round," *Civil War History*, 19 (June 1973), 101–118, ignores the early critics Wilkes, Denslow, and Swinton. Stephen Sears likewise dismissed the early critics in *Controversies & Commanders: Dispatches from the Army of the Potomac* (Boston: Houghton Mifflin, 1999), pp. 3–5. Thomas J. Rowland, *George B. McClellan and Civil War History: In the Shadow of Grant and Sherman* (Kent, Ohio: Kent State University Press, 1998), p. 196, says that Swinton did not have "any particular axes to grind."

58 Fehrenbacher and Fehrenbacher, eds., *Recollected Words of Abraham Lincoln,* p. 446.

59 Unknown lithographer after "Potomac," *Headquarters at Harrison's Landing,* print in the Lincoln Museum, Fort Wayne, Indiana. Harold Holzer and I analyzed political cartoons on this theme in *The Union Image: Popular Prints of the Civil War North* (Chapel Hill: University of North Carolina Press, 2000), pp. 132–151. See also Harold Holzer, *Lincoln Seen and Heard* (Lawrence: University Press of Kansas, 2000), esp. pp. 123–124.

60 "A Collection of the Posters and Broadsides Issued by the Union League of Philadelphia, 1862–1865," Huntington Library, San Marino, California.

61 New York *World,* June 15, 1864.

62 Ibid., June 23, 1864.

63 Ibid., July 7, 1864.

64 Ibid., September 6, 1864.

65 Edwin M. Stanton to Horace Greeley, February 19, 1862, printed in New York *Tribune,* February 20, 1862. See Warren W. Hassler, Jr., *General George B. McClellan: Shield of the Union* (Baton Rouge: Louisiana State University Press, 1957), p. 52, and Benjamin P. Thomas and Harold M. Hyman, *Stanton: The Life and Times of Lincoln's Secretary of War* (New York: Alfred A. Knopf, 1962), p. 174, for differing interpretations of the "Joshua letter."

66 New York *World,* September 6, 1864.

67 Ibid.,

68 David Donald compliments Allan Nevins's foresight in thinking of Union victory as the "organized war" in David H. Donald, ed., *Why the North Won the Civil War* (Baton Rouge, Louisiana: Louisiana State University Press, 1960), p. 9.

4 *"Odious to honourable men"*

1 William Whiting, *The War Powers of the President, and the Legislative Powers of Congress in Relation to Rebellion, Treason and Slavery,* 7th ed. (Boston: John L. Shorey, 1863). Jeffrey A. Smith, *War*

and Press Freedom: The Problem of Prerogative Power (New York: Oxford University Press, 1999), p. 119, reminds us of Whiting's importance in the debate.

2   See Robert Neil Mathis, "Freedom of the Press in the Confederacy: A Reality," *Historian,* 37 (1975), 633–648. See also David H. Donald, "Died of Democracy," in *Why the North Won the Civil War* (Baton Rouge, Louisiana: Louisiana State University Press, 1960), pp. 82–84.

3   Roger Hudson, ed., *William Russell, Special Correspondent of* The Times (London: Folio Society, 1995), p. 222 (diary entry for September 8, 1861).

4   Dated July 23, 1861, in Roy P. Basler, ed., *Collected Works of Abraham Lincoln,* 9 vols. (New Brunswick, New Jersey: Rutgers University Press, 1953–1955), IV, 457.

5   See William Hoffman to George B. McClellan, September 20, 1864, Manton Marble Papers, Library of Congress, container 8.

6   John M. Palmer to Lyman Trumbull, July 24, 1861, with Lincoln endorsement of July 31, in Abraham Lincoln Papers, Library of Congress, microfilm reel 24.

7   New York *Evening Post,* August 26, 27, 1861.

8   Ibid., August 28, 1861.

9   Ibid., August 30, 1861. Lossing dated his letter August 28.

10   New York *Times,* July 29, 1861.

11   Ibid., August 4, 1861.

12   On the old-fashioned doctrine of seditious libel see Leonard Levy, *Jefferson and Civil Liberties: The Darker Side* (1963; Chicago: Ivan R. Dee, 1989), pp. 47–55.

13   New York *Tribune,* August 28, 1861.

14   Ibid., September 9, 1861; Robert S. Harper, *Lincoln and the Press* (New York: McGraw-Hill, 1951), pp. 113–114.

15   Harper, *Lincoln and the Press,* pp. 114–115.

16   William H. Rehnquist, *All the Laws but One: Civil Liberties in Wartime* (New York: Alfred A. Knopf, 1998), pp. 46–47. I follow Rehnquist's description of the case, which is a model of lucid-

ity, and Robert S. Harper, *Lincoln and the Press,* pp. 114-115, for a full delineation of facts.

17 New York *Tribune,* November 7, 1861.

18 Ibid., November 8, 1861. The pioneering constitutional historian James G. Randall imposed a twentieth-century outlook on freedom of the press onto the Civil War era in *Constitutional Problems under Lincoln* (1951; Urbana: University of Illinois Press, 1964), pp. 477-510.

19 Whiting, *The War Powers of the President,* pp. 59-60; John J. Lalor, ed., *Cyclopaedia of Political Science, Political Economy, and of the Political History of the United States,* 3 vols. (1884; New York: Charles E. Merrill, 1893), III, 321.

20 New York *Evening Post,* November 6, 1861.

21 Chicago *Tribune,* August 27, 1861.

22 New York *Evening Post* of August 27, 1861, also quoted Everett. Everett's article was part of a regular column he wrote for the New York *Ledger,* called "Leisure Hours." For his retained copy see Edward Everett Papers, reel 48A.

23 Mark E. Neely, Jr., *The Abraham Lincoln Encyclopedia* (New York: McGraw-Hill, 1982), pp. 56-57.

24 Chicago *Tribune,* June 13, 1863.

25 Ibid., November 17, 1864.

26 Elon Comstock to Abraham Lincoln, June 11, 1863, Abraham Lincoln Papers, microfilm reel 53.

27 New York *Evening Post,* June 9, 1863.

28 New York *Tribune,* July 29, 1864.

29 Ibid., January 26, 1865.

30 Philadelphia *Public Ledger,* July 25, 1864. The New Jersey paper had said that not another man should answer the call, and instead all should defy the president and his "minions to drag them from their families." Dix asserted that such language was unlawful and would lead to "riot"—a sensitive subject when dealing with conscription near New York City in the summer after the previous year's draft riots.

31 Basler, ed., *Coll. Works of Abraham Lincoln,* VI, 266.

32 Philadelphia *Public Ledger,* August 16, 1864.

33 New York *Herald,* July 9, 1864.

34 Ibid., July 10, 1864.

35 Ibid., July 23, 1864.

36 L. H. Funk to Simon Cameron, November 18, 1864, Correspondence and Papers of Simon Cameron, 1824–1892, Historical Society of Dauphin County, microfilm edition by Pennsylvania Historical and Museum Commission, reel 9.

37 Samuel Young to Simon Cameron, November 18, 1862, Simon Cameron Papers, microfilm reel 8.

38 Henry C. Bowen to William H. Seward, August 19, 1862, and to Abraham Lincoln, August 21, 1862, Abraham Lincoln Papers, microfilm reel 40.

39 Henry C. Bowen to William H. Seward, September 24, 1862, Abraham Lincoln Papers, microfilm reel 41.

40 Seward had relinquished personal control of the administration's internal security measures to the War Department the previous February, but he could easily pass the letter along to the secretary of war or to the president for action.

41 Wilkes refused government advertising when Hiram Barney offered it after he, Chase, and other Republicans had noticed Wilkes's work of criticism of McClellan. See George Wilkes to Hamilton Brace, March 28, 1863, Hiram Barney Papers, Huntington Library, San Marino, California, box 30.

42 George Wilkes to Salmon P. Chase, January 31, 1863, Salmon P. Chase Papers, microfilm reel 24.

43 Mark W. Delahay to Abraham Lincoln, June 19, 1863, Abraham Lincoln Papers, microfilm reel 54.

44 William R. Holloway to John G. Nicolay, January 2, 1863, Abraham Lincoln Papers, microfilm reel 47.

45 Emma Lou Thornbrough, *Indiana in the Civil War Era, 1850–1880* (Indianapolis: Indiana Historical Bureau & Indiana Historical Society, 1965), p. 678.

46 Hiram Barney to Salmon P. Chase, September 11, 1862, Salmon P. Chase Papers, microfilm reel 22.

47 Basler, ed., *Coll. Works of Abraham Lincoln,* VIII, 461n.

48 Salmon P. Chase to Henry W. Hoffman, June 15, 1863, Salmon P. Chase Papers, microfilm reel 27.

49 Salmon P. Chase to Hiram Barney, June 17, 1864, Salmon P. Chase Papers, microfilm reel 27.

50 Salmon P. Chase to Hiram Barney, May 17, 1864, Salmon P. Chase Papers, reel 33.

51 Quoted in Manton Marble to William Cassidy, draft letter, July 1864, Manton Marble Papers, container 8.

52 For the facts I rely on Harper, *Lincoln and the Press,* pp. 289–303. George T. McJimsey, *Genteel Partisan: Manton Marble, 1834–1917* (Ames, Iowa: Iowa State University Press, 1971), pp. 52–55, describes the event as one causing a rift between Marble and Seymour.

53 Harper, *Lincoln and the Press,* p. 302.

54 Manton Marble to William Cassidy, draft letter of 12 pages, dated July 1864, in Manton Marble Papers, container 8.

55 See the arguments in *Kneedler v Lane,* 45 Pa. State, 243, 246 (1863).

56 Barlow's letter to Comstock and Cassidy of May 20, 1864, copied in full in Marble's letter of July 1864, Manton Marble Papers, container 8.

57 McJimsey, *Genteel Partisan,* pp. 38–40 (on Barlow's ownership).

5 *"Times of corruption and demoralization"*

1 Goldwin Smith, *Letter to a Whig Member of the Southern Independence Association,* quoted in New York *Evening Post,* May 6, 1864.

2 For the opposite point of view see Leonard P. Curry, "Congressional Democrats, 1861–1863," *Civil War History,* 12 (September 1966), 213–229. Curry argued that the Democrats could not be ignored because their numbers in Congress, though small, were enough to prevent a quorum in the Senate. Curry insisted they could not "be dismissed as politically inconsequential during the Civil War period" (p. 214), that they were

"consistent in their support of the war effort" (p. 229), and that they were "reasoned and responsible in their approach to non-war measures" (p. 229). In short, they "were not extremists" but "an integral and important part of the old political 'center'" (p. 228). The idea of the existence of some nonpartisan "center" hardly makes sense in the extremes of nineteenth-century partisan warfare, and it makes a difference what kind of party activity one examines in assessing the Democrats. Curry does not focus on what was said in debate, on electioneering practice outside Congress, or on the party press.

3 The synthesis most often cited is Joel H. Silbey, *A Respectable Minority: The Democratic Party in the Civil War Era, 1860–1868* (New York: W. W. Norton, 1977). Frank Klement wrote on the peace wing of the party: *The Limits of Dissent: Clement L. Vallandigham and the Civil War* (Lexington: University Press of Kentucky, 1970); *The Copperheads in the Middle West* (Chicago: University of Chicago Press, 1960); and *Dark Lanterns: Secret Political Societies, Conspiracies, and Treason Trials in the Civil War* (Baton Rouge: Louisiana State University Press, 1984). Jean H. Baker's more recent *Affairs of Party: The Political Culture of Northern Democrats in the Mid-Nineteenth Century* (Ithaca: Cornell University Press, 1983) focused as much on American political culture in general as on the peculiar history of the Democrats in the Civil War era.

4 Richard P. McCormick, "Political Development and the Second Party System," in William Nisbet Chambers and Walter Dean Burnham, eds., *The American Party Systems: Stages of Political Development* (New York: Oxford University Press, 1967), p. 95. The party systems-realigning elections school of interpretation championed in that book was particularly effective in making comparisons over long periods of time.

5 James M. Banner, Jr., *To the Hartford Convention: The Federalists and the Origins of Party Politics in Massachusetts, 1789–1815* (New York: Alfred A. Knopf, 1970), pp. 341–342.

6 David M. Potter, "Jefferson Davis and the Political Factors in Confederate Defeat," in David H. Donald, ed., *Why the North Won the Civil War* (Baton Rouge: Louisiana State University Press, 1960), pp. 114.

7 *Cong. Globe,* 38 Cong., 1 sess., p. 467; 2 sess., pp. 421, 439; Appendix, pp. 103–108.

8 Michael F. Holt reminded us of the "embarrassing presence of strident antiwar Democrats such as Ohio's Clement L. Vallandigham, Pennsylvania's George W. Woodward, and Connecticut's Thomas Seymour, all of whom captured Democratic gubernatorial nominations in 1863" in "An Elusive Synthesis," p. 123.

9 Basler, ed., *Coll. Works of Abraham Lincoln,* VIII, 332–333.

10 Eric L. McKitrick, "Party Politics and the Union and Confederate War Efforts," p. 142.

11 Harrisburg *Patriot and Union,* February 13, 1864.

12 For the reaction in the Confederacy to their camps of instruction see the chapter on "Alcohol and Martial Law" in Mark E. Neely, Jr., *Southern Rights: Political Prisoners and the Myth of Confederate Constitutionalism* (Charlottesville: University Press of Virginia, 1999).

13 Harrisburg *Patriot and Union,* March 2, 1864.

14 Ibid., March 3, 1864.

15 Ibid., March 4, 1864.

16 See for example ibid., March 5 and 7, 1864.

17 The thugs were called in contemporary slang "knucks." See ibid., March 9, 1864.

18 Ibid., March 11, 1864.

19 That is the interpretive scheme that informs the standard work on the wartime Democratic party, Silbey's *A Respectable Minority,* which depicted Democratic politics as a struggle between "Purists," who wanted to emphasize the party's historic ideology, and "Legitimists," who wanted to take measures to maximize the party's vote-getting ability.

20 William Dusinberre, *Civil War Issues in Philadelphia, 1856–1865* (Philadelphia: University of Pennsylvania Press, 1965), pp. 149–187. On p. 187 Dusinberre, impressed with the extremism of the Democrats in Philadelphia, said, "Considering the vigor of the Democratic opposition to Republican measures, and remembering the inadequate volunteering, the great number of deserters, and the necessity for military precautions against draft rioting, one must ask how much Democratic hostility to administration policies may have contributed to the catastrophic way in which the North conducted the war."

21 The ineptitude and pro-Southern extremism of the Democratic party in Philadelphia left that city without an able and widely circulated Democratic newspaper. The Democratic paper in the state capital was more important than it may appear, therefore. On Philadelphia and the weak circulation of the Democratic *Age,* see C. L. Ward to Manton Marble, September 30,1864, Manton Marble Papers, Library of Congress, container 9.

22 Quoted in the Harrisburg *Patriot and Union,* March 22, 1864.

23 Ibid., March 22, 1864.

24 Quoted in the Harrisburg *Patriot and Union,* March 30, 1864. See Bernard Bailyn, *The Ideological Origins of the American Revolution* (Cambridge: Harvard University Press, 1967), pp. 36, 132.

25 Harrisburg *Patriot and Union,* April 16, 1864.

26 Quoting the Philadelphia *Public Ledger* in the Harrisburg *Patriot and Union,* April 24, 1864.

27 See for example the Harrisburg *Patriot and Union,* May 3 and 14, 1864.

28 Ibid., May 17, 1864.

29 Ibid., June 24, 1864.

30 David B. Davis, "Some Themes of Countersubversion: An Analysis of Anti-Masonic, Anti-Catholic, and Anti-Mormon Literature," *Mississippi Valley Historical Review,* 47 (September 1960), 217. The article was reprinted with documents from

American history illustrating the theme in Davis, *The Fear of Conspiracy: Images of Un-American Subversion from the Revolution to the Present* (Ithaca: Cornell University Press, 1971).

31 Harrisburg *Patriot and Union,* July 15, 1864.

32 Ibid., June 21, 1864.

33 On "political culture" see Baker, *Affairs of Party,* esp. chapter 7, "The Meaning of Elections." Michael F. Holt expresses "doubt that a focus on political culture provides a practicable way to synthesize the literature on Civil War politics." Holt, "An Elusive Synthesis," p. 127.

34 Joel H. Silbey, ed., *The American Party Battle: Election Campaign Pamphlets, 1828–1876,* 2 vols. (Cambridge: Harvard University Press, 1999), II, xviii, xix.

35 New York *World,* March 7, 1863.

36 Frank L. Klement, *The Limits of Dissent: Clement L. Vallandigham and the Civil War* (1970; New York: Fordham University Press, 1998), p. 277.

37 Harrisburg *Patriot and Union,* April 24, 1864.

38 See Harrisburg *Telegraph,* March 31, 1864; April 2, 4, and 7, 1864; *The Legislative Record Containing the Debates . . . of the Pennsylvania Legislature in the Session of 1864* (Harrisburg: Telegraph Job Office, 1864), pp. 352, 781.

39 I rely on Fred Niklason, "The Civil War Contracts Committee," *Civil War History,* 17 (September 1971), 232–244. For a somewhat different view of such committees as politically motivated but dysfunctional for party unity, see Allan G. Bogue, *The Congressman's Civil War* (New York: Cambridge University Press, 1989), pp. 60–109.

40 See, for example, New York *World,* February 13 and 21, 1863.

41 Henry Morford, *The Days of Shoddy: A Novel of the Great Rebellion in 1861* (Philadelphia: T. B. Peterson, 1863), p. 178. For Morford's support of Lincoln see his novel *Red-Tape and Pigeon-Hole Generals: As Seen from the Ranks during a Campaign in the Army of the Potomac* (New York: Carleton, 1864), preface and p. 189.

42 See Michael F. Holt, *The Rise and Fall of the American Whig Party: Jacksonian Politics and the Onset of the Civil War* (New York: Oxford University Press, 1999), pp. 212, 349.

43 Information on Burr comes from Joseph George, Jr., "'Abraham Africanus I': President Lincoln through the Eyes of a Copperhead Editor," *Civil War History*, 14 (September 1968), 226-239.

44 "History of Northern Disunion," *The Old Guard*, 2 (November 1864), 241-246; "The Old Monarchist Party of the United States," *The Old Guard*, 2 (December 1864), 265-273.

45 *The Old Guard*, 2 (June 1864), 144.

46 Ibid., 140.

6 *"Paroxysms of rage and fear"*

1 See, for example, John Morton Blum, *V Was for Victory: Politics and American Culture during World War II* (New York: Harcourt, Brace, Jovanovich, 1976).

2 Mark E. Neely, Jr., *The Last Best Hope of Earth: Abraham Lincoln and the Promise of America* (Cambridge: Harvard University Press, 1993), p. 141.

3 See David M. Kennedy, *Over Here: The First World War and American Society* (New York: Oxford University Press, 1980), pp. 97-98, 141-143, 245-258.

4 The panic of 1873 served to send economic issues into prominence with Republicans. See especially Eric Foner, *Reconstruction: America's Unfinished Revolution, 1863–1877* (New York: Harper & Row, 1988), pp. 512-534.

5 See J. Matthew Gallman and Stanley Engermann, "The Civil War Economy: A Modern View," in Stig Forster and Jorg Nagler, eds., *On the Road to Total War: The American Civil War and the German Wars of Unification, 1861–1871* (Cambridge: Cambridge University Press, 1997), pp. 217-248, and Richard Franklin Bensel, *Yankee Leviathan: The Origins of Central State Authority in America, 1859–1877* (Cambridge: Cambridge University Press, 1990), esp. pp. 183-188.

6 See Eric Foner, *Free Soil, Free Labor, Free Men: The Ideology of the Republican Party before the Civil War* (New York: Oxford University Press, 1970), p. 31.

7 Although he does not carry the idea forward to the Civil War and confines his analysis to the ideas of Abraham Lincoln without looking at the Republican party as a whole, Stewart Winger in "Lincoln's Economics and the American Dream: A Reappraisal," *Journal of the Abraham Lincoln Association,* 22 (2001), 51–80, offers a brilliant critique of Foner and influenced me heavily to reconsider the idea of free labor in Republican political ideas during the later Civil War period.

8 Charleston *Mercury,* February 12, 1862 (letter from the New Orleans correspondent dated February 5).

9 Charleston *Courier,* August 12, 1862.

10 Richmond *Dispatch,* April 8, 1864.

11 Richmond *Dispatch,* April 23, 1864. The first to identify belief among northern intellectuals in the southern critique of capitalism was William R. Taylor in *Cavalier and Yankee: The Old South and American National Character* (1961; Garden City: Doubleday, 1963). Michael C. C. Adams carried the idea forward in a way in *Fighting for Defeat: Union Military Failure in the East, 1861-1865* (orig. pub. as *Our Masters the Rebels,* 1978; Lincoln: University of Nebraska Press, 1992).

12 Quoted in Frank Freidel, ed., *Union Pamphlets of the Civil War, 1861–1865,* 2 vols. (Cambridge: Harvard University Press, 1967), I, 17.

13 Oliver P. Morton to Abraham Lincoln, October 7, 1862, Abraham Lincoln Papers, Library of Congress, microfilm reel 42.

14 Fred Niklason, "The Civil War Contracts Committee," *Civil War History,* 17 (September 1971), 239.

15 Horace Porter, *Campaigning with Grant* (1897; Lincoln: University of Nebraska Press, 2000), p. 359.

16 Foner, *Free Soil, Free Labor, Free Men,* pp. 50, 59.

17 "The Ordeal by Battle," *Atlantic Monthly,* 8 (July 1861), 90. For similar statements see the New York *Times,* September 1, 1861

("They have so long depended upon the North for these [supplies of powder and ball], that they have neither the skill or materials for their fabrication"), September 10, 1861 ("their utter poverty and nakedness is exposed to the glare of the world"), and September 22, 1861 ("With such poverty on one side and wealth on the other, there can be no more doubt about the result than can be due to any natural law"). See especially "The Greasy Mechanic in a New Light," September 30, 1861, and C. G. Leland, "The Crisis and the Parties," *Continental Monthly*, 2 (July 1862), 65–69. For an affirmation of the superiority of northern capitalism late in the war see "The Resources North and South, or the Two Civilizations," New York *Evening Post*, January 27, 1864.

18 New York *Tribune*, August 8, 1861.

19 New York *Evening Post*, July 21, 1862.

20 David M. Potter, *The Impending Crisis, 1848–1861* (New York: Harper & Row, 1976), pp. 373–375.

21 New York *Tribune*, October 14, 1861.

22 New York *Evening Post*, July 21, 1862. This is part of the article on "The South as a War Power" cited above. The *Evening Post* could not resist reminding its readers of another deceptive advantage of the Confederacy, the party divisions in the North: "That the South has a material war power within the northern states, from which it derives aid and comfort, is incontestible."

23 New York *Tribune*, October 23, 1861.

24 Roy P. Basler, ed., *The Collected Works of Abraham Lincoln*, 9 vols. (New Brunswick, New Jersey: Rutgers University Press, 1953–1955), V, 51–52. See esp. Stewart Winger, "Lincoln's Economics and the American Dream: A Reappraisal," *Journal of the Abraham Lincoln Association*, 22 (2001), 60–80; Gabor S. Boritt, *Lincoln and the Economics of the American Dream* (1978; Urbana: University of Illinois Press, 1994).

25 Horace Greeley, *The American Conflict: A History of the Great Rebellion . . . Intended to Exhibit Its Moral and Political Phases*, 2 vols.

(Hartford: O. D. Case, 1864), I, 499. I explore this idea further in "'Civilized Belligerents': Abraham Lincoln and the Idea of Total War," in John Y. Simon and Michael E. Stevens, eds., *New Perspectives on the Civil War: Myths and Realities of the National Conflict* (Madison: Madison House, 1998), pp. 3-8.

26 Leonard P.Curry, *Blueprint for Modern America* (Nashville, Tenn.: Vanderbilt University Press, 1968) and Heather Cox Richardson, *The Greatest Nation of the Earth: Republican Economic Policies during the Civil War* (Cambridge: Harvard University Press, 1997).

27 I borrow the tripartite analysis of political party from Ronald P. Formisano, "Deferential-Participant Politics: The Early Republic's Political Culture, 1789-1840," *American Political Science Review,* 68 (1974), 473-487.

28 Elihu B. Washburne to Abraham Lincoln, October 17, 1864, Abraham Lincoln Papers, microfilm reel 84.

29 As far as we know. Edgar Conkling to Abraham Lincoln, October 8, 1864, Abraham Lincoln Papers, microfilm reel 83, and Isaac Langworthy to Edgar Conkling, October 17, 1864, Abraham Lincoln Papers, reel 84.

30 President Lincoln was sent printed circulars Train drew up after the Democratic convention in Chicago. See his "Letter to McClellan" and "Train's Third Manifesto" at August 31, 1864 in the Abraham Lincoln Papers, microfilm reel 80.

31 Philadelphia *Inquirer,* October 28 and 31, 1864.

32 Ibid., October 31, 1864.

33 William Cullen Bryant, II, and Thomas G. Voss, *The Letters of William Cullen Bryant, Volume IV, 1858–1864* (New York: Fordham University Press, 1984), p. 371.

34 For the most anti-Semitic editorial see Harrisburg *Telegraph,* October 31, 1864. See also November 7, 1864.

35 Philadelphia *Inquirer,* October 28, 1864.

36 Ibid., November 1, 1864. For reactions see October 28, 1864 and Harrisburg *Telegraph,* November 8, 1864.

37 *Speech of Aaron F. Perry, Esq., Delivered before the National Union*

Association, at Mozart Hall, Cincinnati, Sept. 20, 1864 (Cincinnati, Ohio: Caleb Clark, [1864]), p. 13; excerpted in the New York *Evening Post,* October 27, 1864.

38 See Halsted to Lincoln, October 1, 1864, Abraham Lincoln papers, microfilm reel 83, and George Wilkes to Halsted, copies of September 27 and 30 at the 27th date in the Abraham Lincoln Papers, microfilm reel 82.

39 He may not have noticed that the *Evening Post* reprinted Aaron F. Perry's attack on Belmont.

40 New York *Evening Post,* November 22, 1864. Wolf's letter was dated November 20.

41 New York *World,* October 5, 1864.

42 Arthur M. Schlesinger, Jr., and Fred L. Israel, eds., *History of American Presidential Elections, 1789-1968,* 4 vols. (New York: Chelsea House, 1971), II, 1179.

43 Ibid., II, 1040, 1043.

44 Philadelphia *Public Ledger,* September 26, 1864.

45 New York *Evening Post,* November 10, 1864. The *Evening Post* thought press freedom prevented "more serious collisions" by serving as "escape valves for the high pressure of passion which party conflicts are apt to generate. They let off the steam, and when that is done, the machinery works with its accustomed regularity."

46 New York *Tribune,* September 18, 1862.

47 James R. Gilmore to Abraham Lincoln, July 17, 1863, Abraham Lincoln Papers, microfilm reel 55.

48 Edmunds to James R. Gilmore, July 21, 1863, Abraham Lincoln Papers, microfilm reel 56.

49 Gilmore to Abraham Lincoln, July 26, 1863, Abraham Lincoln Papers, microfilm reel 56. The incident is not mentioned in Iver Bernstein's *The New York City Draft Riots: Their Significance for American Society and Politics in the Age of the Civil War* (New York: Oxford University Press, 1990).

50 New York *Tribune,* July 29, 1864.

51 Ibid., August 3, 1864.

52 Ibid., August 13, 1864.

53 Frank L. Klement, *Dark Lanterns: Secret Political Societies, Conspiracies, and Treason Trials in the Civil War* (Baton Rouge, Louisiana: Louisiana State University Press, 1984), p. 136.

54 For dates of release of the report see Frank L. Klement, *Dark Lanterns,* esp. p. 145. Klement nevertheless believed it a Republican fabrication and dirty trick.

55 New York *Evening Post,* August 1, 1864.

56 Ibid., October 15, 1864.

57 Ibid., October 19, 1864.

58 New York *Times,* July 30, 1864.

59 Ibid., September 22, October 16, 1864.

60 Harrisburg *Telegraph,* February 23, 1864.

61 See ibid., February 22 and 27, March 3 and 9, December 3, 1864.

62 Ibid., August 23 and September 15, 1864.

63 Ibid., September 15, 1864.

64 New York *Times,* October 5, 1864.

65 Chicago *Tribune,* July 29, 1864. See also, for example, August 9.

66 Alfred H. Kelly, Winfred Harbison, and Herman Belz, *The American Constitution: Its Origins and development,* 2 vols. (seventh ed.; New York: W. W. Norton, 1991), I, 317. See also Harold M. Hyman, "Election of 1864," in Arthur M. Schlesinger, Jr., and Fred L. Israel, eds., *History of American Presidential Elections, 1789–1968,* 4 vols. (New York: Chelsea House, 1971), II, 1176: "The upshot of 1864 was a consensus, not about the nature of a rewon Union, but about the validity of continuing two-party politics and regular elections to decide that nature."

67 Basler, ed., *Coll. Works of Abraham Lincoln,* VIII, 101.

68 Harrisburg *Telegraph,* November 12, 1864.

69 Ibid., November 10, 1864.

70 Ibid., November 23, 1864.

71 New York *World,* November 10, 1864.

72 Salmon P. Chase to Jay Cooke, November 10, 1864, Salmon P. Chase Papers, microfilm reel 35.

73 Salmon P. Chase to William Dennison, November 11, 1864, Salmon P. Chase Papers, microfilm reel 35.

74 Chicago *Tribune,* November 10, 1864.

75 Ibid., December 8, 1864.

76 New York *Times,* November 13, 1864.

77 Ibid., November 25, 1864.

78 Philadelphia *Inquirer,* November 17, 1864.

79 (New York: Alfred A. Knopf, 2000), p. 16.

80 Page 187. George C. Rable was also struck by the analogy to the early republic's party conflicts. See *The Confederate Republic: A Revolution against Politics* (Chapel Hill: University of North Carolina Press, 1994), 144.

7 *The Civil War and the Two-Party System*

1 The terms "political nation" and "partisan imperative" come from the work of Joel Silbey but stand here for a whole school of interpretation of nineteenth-century politics. See Silbey, *The American Political Nation, 1838–1893* (Stanford: Stanford University Press, 1991), p. 139, for example.

2 George M. Fredrickson, *The Inner Civil War: Northern Intellectuals and the Crisis of the Union* (New York: Harper & Row, 1965), esp. chap. 9.

3 George C. Rable, *The Confederate Republic: A Revolution against Politics* (Chapel Hill: University of North Carolina Press, 1994), pp. 131, 144, for example.

4 David M. Potter, "Jefferson Davis and the Political Factors in Confederate Defeat," in David H. Donald, ed., *Why the North Won the Civil War* (Baton Rouge: Louisiana State University Press, 1960), p. 113.

5 Eric McKitrick, "Party Politics and the Union and Confederate War Efforts," in William Nisbet Chambers and Walter Dean Burnham, eds., *The American Party Systems: Stages of De-*

velopment (New York: Oxford University Press, 1967), p. 120. See also Daniel W. Crofts, review of Rable, *The Confederate Republic,* in *American Historical Review,* 101 (December 1995), 1685–1686.

6 Michael F. Holt, "Abraham Lincoln and the Politics of Union," in John L. Thomas, ed., *Abraham Lincoln and the American Political Tradition* (Amherst: University of Massachusetts Press, 1986), p. 111.

7 James M. McPherson, *Ordeal by Fire: The Civil War and Reconstruction* (New York: Alfred A. Knopf, 1982), p. 368.

8 James M. McPherson, *Battle Cry of Freedom: The Civil War Era* (New York: Oxford University Press, 1988), p. 690.

9 Phillip Shaw Paludan, *"A People's Contest": The Union and Civil War, 1861–1865* (New York: Harper & Row, 1988), pp. 89, 378.

10 Alfred H. Kelly, Winfred A. Harbison, and Herman Belz, *The American Constitution: Its Origins and Development,* 2 vols. (7th ed.; New York: W. W. Norton, 1991), I, 317.

11 Michael F. Holt, "An Elusive Synthesis: Northern Politics during the Civil War," in James M. McPherson and William J. Cooper, Jr., eds., *Writing the Civil War: The Quest to Understand* (Columbia: University of South Carolina Press, 1998), pp. 117, 118. Rable calls the "main arguments . . . deceptively simple and plausible" in *The Confederate Republic,* p. 120.

12 Gary W. Gallagher, *The Confederate War* (Cambridge: Harvard University Press, 1997); William Blair, *Virginia's Private War: Feeding Body and Soul in the Confederacy, 1861–1865* (New York: Oxford University Press, 1998); Rable, *The Confederate Republic.*

13 See E. E. Schattschneider, *Party Government* (New York: Rinehart, 1942), p. 1; Sigmund Neumann, ed., *Modern Political Parties: Approaches to Comparative Politics* (Chicago: University of Chicago Press, 1956), p. 1. See also William Nisbet Chambers, "Party Development and the American Mainstream," in Chambers and Walter Dean Burnham, eds., *The American Party Systems: Stages of Political Development* (New York: Oxford

University Press, 1967), pp. 7–8, for expression of the view that parties "have tended to contain or resolve political conflict more than they have tended to intensify or exacerbate it." He points even to the "significant integrative functions" of the Federalist and Republican parties, which gave American history the Alien and Sedition Act, originated the theory of nullification, and flirted with secession.

14 See especially J. Mills Thornton, III, *Politics and Power in a Slave Society: Alabama, 1800–1860* (Baton Rouge: Louisiana State University Press, 1978), and Michael F. Holt, *The Political Crisis of the 1850s* (New York: W. W. Norton, 1978).

15 Holt, "An Elusive Synthesis," p. 118.

16 See, for example, W. Buck Yearns, ed., *The Confederate Governors* (Athens: University of Georgia Press, 1985). Both presidents faced insuperable difficulties in dealing with border states—Lincoln with Missouri, and Davis with East Tennessee and western Virginia. Michael Fellman's *Inside War: The Guerrilla Conflict in Missouri during the American Civil War* (New York: Oxford University press, 1989) was the first book to revise the image of Lincoln as a master of border state relations. For a reminder of Davis's failures with border states see Mark E. Neely, Jr., *Southern Rights: Political Prisoners and the Myth of Confederate Constitutionalism* (Charlottesville: University Press of Virginia, 1999), esp. pp. 99–133.

17 The "conflict between parties in Indiana temporarily destroyed constitutional government, and made Morton as much a dictator as Charles I," wrote Allan Nevins in *The War for the Union: Volume II, War Becomes Revolution, 1862–1863* (New York: Charles Scribner's Sons, 1960), p. 392. Kenneth Stampp described it a "the collapse of constitutional government" in *Indiana Politics during the Civil War* (1949; Bloomington: Indiana University Press, 1978), p. 158. James G. Randall termed the situation in Illinois and Indiana "a collapse of representative government" in *Lincoln the President: Midstream* (New York: Dodd, Mead, 1954), p. 253. This book has ignored the fractious

politics of the border states, but it is worth keeping in mind that Michael Fellman, for example, described the Union takeover of Missouri's state government as a "coup d'etat" in *Inside War*, p. 10.

18 Eugene Converse Murdock, *Patriotism Limited, 1862–1865: The Civil War Draft and the Bounty System* (Kent, Ohio: Kent State University Press, 1967), p. 4.

19 Ibid., p. 10. Only 9,881 men were conscripted from the whole nation, with another 26,002 drafted men paying for substitutes to serve in their stead. No calculation exists for the New York draft call alone, but see the figures for the 14th district where 1,000 soldiers and a section of artillery oversaw the 1863 draft in a district that supplied for all draft calls in the war only 49 drafted men and 4,764 paying for substitutes. *The War of the Rebellion: A Compilation of the Official Records of the Union and Confederate Armies*, 128 vols. (Washington, D.C.: Government Printing Office, 1880–1902), ser. III, vol. 3, pp. 723, 825. For rejections see pp. 1058–1059. See Murdock, *Patriotism Limited*, p. 210. For correspondence, see, for example, a list, written by Provost Marshal General James B. Fry, of contacts between the Provost Marshal General and the president with Governor Seymour and his agents at October 31, 1863, in the Abraham Lincoln Papers, Library of Congress, microfilm reel 62. For evidence of problems with Democratic Governor Joel Parker of New Jersey see, for example, James B. Fry to Robert C. Buchanan, at same date.

20 McKitrick, "Party Politics and the Union and Confederate War Efforts," p. 150.

21 Ibid., p. 151.

22 These terms appear in Richard Hofstadter, *The Paranoid Style in American Politics* (New York: Alfred A. Knopf, 1965); David Brion Davis, "Some Themes of Countersubversion: An Analysis of Anti-Masonic, Anti-Catholic, and Anti-Mormon Literature," *Mississippi Valley Historical Review*, 67 (September 1960), 205-224; David Brion Davis, *The Slave Power Conspiracy and the*

Paranoid Style (Baton Rouge: Louisiana State University Press, 1969); and (the last two phrases quoted in the series) Holt, *The Political Crisis of the 1850s*, p. 5.

23 McKitrick, "Party Politics and the Union and Confederate War Efforts," p. 141.

24 Gordon Wood, "Conspiracy and the Paranoid Style: Causality and Deceit in the Eighteenth Century," *William and Mary Quarterly*, 39 (January 1982), 404-441.

25 See Heather Cox Richardson, *The Greatest Nation of the Earth: Republican Economic Policies during the Civil War* (Cambridge: Harvard University Press, 1997), pp. 15-27.

26 Jacob E. Cooke, ed., *The Federalist* (Middletown, Connecticut: Wesleyan University Press, 1961), p. 349.

27 Wood, "Conspiracy and the Paranoid Style," pp. 401-441. Wood does not examine the problem of party in the context, and he goes a little too far in separating the world view from irrationality.

28 Phillip Shaw Paludan, *"A People's Contest": The Union and Civil War, 1861–1865* (New York: Harper & Row, 1988), p. 378.

29 McKitrick, "Party Politics and the Union and Confederate War Efforts," p. 144.

30 Michael F. Holt, "Abraham Lincoln and the Politics of Union," in John L. Thomas, ed., *Abraham Lincoln and the American Political Tradition* (Amherst: University of Massachusetts Press, 1986), pp. 112-113.

31 A valuable contrasting image of party government in this era can be found in Richard Franklin Bensel, *Yankee Leviathan: The Origin of Central State Authority in America, 1859–1877* (Cambridge: Cambridge University Press, 1990).

32 For an example of carrying the two-party-system theory so far as to glorify the patronage system, see Paludan, *"A People's Contest,"* p. 378: "It also opened careers and patronage to those ambitious men who played by the rules."

33 Bensel, *Yankee Leviathan,* pp. 236-237. Although he devoted pp. 228-237 to consideration of parts of the two-party-system

theory, Bensel showed surprisingly little interest in the argument. He seems skeptical of its explanatory value, especially for the Confederacy.

34 On this point, my information comes from Michael F. Holt in seminar at the Civil War Era Center, Pennsylvania State University, April 12, 2001. I am grateful to Professor Holt for the help.

35 I borrow the language of Mark Grimsley, *The Hard Hand of War: Union Military Policy toward Southern Civilians, 1861–1865* (New York: Cambridge University Press, 1995).

36 This shaping constitutional factor should be added to those enumerated by Gary W. Gallagher in *The Confederate War* (Cambridge: Harvard University Press, 1997), pp. 126–142. For other considerations see Joseph Harsh, Jr., *Confederate Tide Rising: Robert E. Lee and the Making of Southern Strategy, 1861-1862* (Kent, OH: Kent State University Press, 1998).

37 Colin R. Ballard, *The Military Genius of Abraham Lincoln* (1926; Cleveland, Ohio: World Publishing, 1952), p. 13.

38 Joel H. Silbey, *A Respectable Minority: The Democratic Party in the Civil War Era, 1860–1868* (New York: W. W. Norton, 1977), pp. 20–22; William Best Hesseltine, *Lincoln and the War Governors* (New York: Alfred A. Knopf, 1948); Leonard P. Curry, *Blueprint for Modern America: Nonmilitary Legislation of the First Civil War Congress* (Nashville: Vanderbilt University Press, 1968), p. 34. Some party names and identifications were vague in the flux of parties, so the number of Democrats stated varies from 44–49.

39 Curry, *Blueprint for Modern America,* pp. 253-254; Leonard P. Curry, "Congressional Democrats, 1861-1863," *Civil War History,* 12 (September 1966), 214. Because the numbers remained unadjusted after the resignation of the southerners to the Confederacy, 35 was required for a quorum in the Senate, and the Republicans, Curry points out, never mustered that number in the 37th Congress.

40 Abraham Lincoln to Carl Schurz, November 10, 1862, in
    Basler, ed., *Coll. Works of Abraham Lincoln*, V, 494.
41 See Michael Fellman, *Inside War: The Guerrilla Conflict in Missouri during the American Civil War* (New York: Oxford University Press, 1989), esp. p. 10.
42 McKitrick, "Party Politics and the Union and Confederate War Efforts," pp. 144–145. I was gratified by constitutional historian Brian Dirck's agreement on this point, expressed in the symposium "Abraham Lincoln: Myth an Image," South Bend, Indiana, March 31, 2001.

INDEX